A Scamper Through America

T. S. Hudson

Contents

INTRODUCTION. 7

A SCAMPER THROUGH AMERICA. 7

DAY ONE. 7

DAY TWO. 9

DAY THREE. 11

DAY FOUR. 13

DAY FIVE. 14

DAY SIX. 15

DAY SEVEN. 16

DAY EIGHT. 16

DAY NINE. 17

DAY TEN. 18

DAY ELEVEN. 21

DAY TWELVE. 25

DAY THIRTEEN. 27

DAY FOURTEEN. 27

DAY FIFTEEN. 28

DAY SIXTEEN. 29

DAY SEVENTEEN. 30

DAY EIGHTEEN. 32

DAY NINETEEN. 33

DAY TWENTY. 37

DAY TWENTY-ONE. 39

DAY TWENTY-TWO. 40

DAY TWENTY-THREE. 43

DAY TWENTY-FOUR. 44

DAY TWENTY-FIVE. 45

DAY TWENTY-SIX. 49

DAY TWENTY-SEVEN. 52

DAY TWENTY-EIGHT. 56

DAY TWENTY-NINE. 59

DAY THIRTY. 63

DAY THIRTY-ONE. 69

DAY THIRTY-TWO. 71

DAY THIRTY-THREE. 74

DAY THIRTY FOUR. 77

DAY THIRTY-FIVE. 79

DAY THIRTY-SIX. 82

DAY THIRTY-SEVEN. 84

DAY THIRTY-EIGHT. 87

DAY THIRTY-NINE. 89

DAY FORTY. 91

DAY FORTY-ONE. 92

DAY FORTY-TWO. 94

DAY FORTY-THREE. 99

DAY FORTY-FOUR. 102

DAY FORTY-FIVE. 104

DAY FORTY-SIX. 105

DAY FORTY-SEVEN. 108

DAY FORTY-EIGHT. 110

DAY FORTY-NINE. 111

DAY FIFTY. 115
DAY FIFTY-ONE. 118
DAY FIFTY-TWO. 120
DAY FIFTY-THREE. 121
DAY FIFTY-FOUR. 122
DAY FIFTY-FIVE. 124
DAY FIFTY-SIX. 126
DAY FIFTY-SEVEN. 126
DAY FIFTY-EIGHT. 127
DAY FIFTY-NINE. 127
DAY SIXTY. 128

A SCAMPER THROUGH AMERICA

BY

T. S. Hudson

INTRODUCTION.

A description of the voyages to and from, and a tour in, America, may appear to be the telling of a more than thrice-told tale; but, with all previous knowledge acquired by reading, one finds upon coming to have personal experience of such a journey that there is enough to fill volumes with facts and impressions that other, and more literary, travellers have not thought it worth while to narrate.

A SCAMPER THROUGH AMERICA.
DAY ONE.

In the first hour of the day, it being past midnight, we left behind the lightship at the bar of the river Mersey, being bound for New York on board the good Inman steamship **City of Rome.** Vexatious delays following upon a needlessly early embarkation, insisted upon by the Company owning the vessel, had caused my wife and myself to be heartily thankful when the vessel's moorings off New Brighton were quitted, and the glimmering gas jets and bright flame of the lighthouse were at last lost sight of. When fairly out at sea we were quickly in the arms of Morpheus, ensconsed in the "berths" which were to be our more or less delightful couches during the nights of the next week or more.

A very few hours of sleep satisfied me on this Good Friday morning, for the consciousness of speeding on towards the great Atlantic pervaded even my dreams, and prompted a rush on deck with the first waking moments. The crew were already busy lowering into the hold the heaps of multifarious luggage which lumbered the decks, the inextricable confusion giving promise of the vexation of spirit that the sorting-out was to occasion at the journey's end. What a contrast to my last celebration of this marked day of the Church's calendar, when about the same hour of the morning I had come on deck in the Black Sea and found myself surrounded by a motley company of Orientals, refugees from the earthquaked island of Chios, bound for the Danube in search of fresh fields and pastures new!

I was called from my involuntary reverting to a year agone by the appearing ahead upon the smooth sea of what appeared to be an island, which as we approached proved to be the rock of Tuscar, covered with turf and crowned with its snow-white lighthouse. This is the southeasternmost outpost of Ireland, and a few miles further on we hailed the Saltees lightship, which also tells the mariner how near he may safely "hug" this corner of the Emerald Isle.

The wind was east, and it would be cold enough in many parts of Great Britain that April morning, but going as we were with the breeze, and the bright sun glinting upon the surface of the water, it felt absolutely warm. The biggest ship afloat, barring the ***Great Eastern,*** steamed on at the rate of seventeen knots an hour, with so little heaving or vibration that writing with pen and ink was as easy and steady a performance as at a desk in the library at home.

At three o'clock we entered the beautiful Cove of Cork, and, in full view of Queenstown and its picturesque surroundings, dropped anchor to await the mails. But there was business to be done. Our cargo was not all on board, neither was our complement of passengers yet achieved. Tons of potatoes were quickly handed up from craft alongside, and hundreds of Irish emigrants stepped along a plank from the paddle-box of the tender to join the passengers in our comfortable steerage.

Never was vessel built with such ample accommodation for all classes of those who travel by water; and her reputation by this her second voyage had already sufficiently spread to attract an overflowing company of crossers to the New World. Some good-natured jostling, amounting at times to rough horseplay, took place as the new contingent crowded up the gangway; and some amusing, as well as affecting, leave-takings took place.

Every man had his shillalagh, and the women had good tangled heads of hair, innocent of any hat or bonnet. Take them altogether they were a jovial crew, and were in high spirits at setting out to make a fresh start in life; leaving old Ireland and its troubles behind.

Being a close holiday in Cork we were honoured with boatloads of visitors; steamers and smaller craft, gay with bunting, hovering around.

Before the tender left us a large traffic was carried on in oranges, lemons, apples, and sweets, the money being first passed down in a basket, which was then returned laden with the ***quid pro quo.*** This, however, over, the passengers amused themselves by throwing money for the girls who had come off in the tender to scramble for, and this proved a much more remunerative occupation for the buxom Irish lasses than the more legitimate one of selling fruit; for shillings were showered down upon them in lavish profusion. The women, both those who remained and those who returned to the shore, were a better sample than the men, being strong and burly and more equal to the occasion than their male companions.

At seven o'clock we passed Cape Clear and saw the sun set over a still more westerly point of land that loomed far away over our starboard bow. A very auspicious farewell to land it was, for the sky was clear and bright, and a bark in full sail crossing the last streaks of sunlight on the sea furnished a picture, which, with the dark hills for a background, was one of singular beauty. Hundreds of seagulls were drawn after us in the deepening twilight by the ***debris*** of victuals thrown over the ship's side, and by a young lady, who, with a plate of bread, stood by the taffrail and threw morsels into the waves, which caused the hungry birds to swoop in ones, twos, and dozens to cleverly snap, or voraciously scramble for, the tit-bits, which with marvellous quickness of sight they espied.

DAY TWO.

With the wind blowing east-south-east, the weather bright and fine, and smooth sea, we sped on our course, which was now set due west. At ten o'clock in the forenoon the log was cast and indicated that we were going at a speed of fifteen and a half knots per hour. (Six knots are equal to about seven statute miles.)

There are patent logs, which, being drawn in the vessel's wake, register the number of revolutions made by the instrument in its passage through the water, and so the distance is recorded with sufficient accuracy; but in the present case the old-fashioned canvas bag and line were used at stated intervals during the day. The bag being thrown into the sea remains stationary, while its attached string runs out from a reel and a sand-glass is being run. Bits of coloured bunting are knotted on the line, and according to which of these is reached by the time the glass has marked its number of seconds the speed can be calculated to a nicety. The realing-in of the log is no easy task, and is only rendered possible, without requiring an awkwardly heavy rope to avoid breaking, by a contrivance which causes the "bag" to be reversed and cease holding the water, as soon as the check is applied to the line. Watching this operation was a favourite pastime.

At eight o'clock in the morning and at noon the captain and officers took their "observations" which proved exactly where the ship was, and each mid-day the number of miles traversed was posted in the saloon, and the position marked upon a chart, an elegant duplicate of which (upon the back of which was a printed list of the passengers) was in the possession of each of us. In an absence of the sun the periodical records of the log are an invaluable guide as to the steamer's whereabouts.

The propellor, or "screw," was revolving at the rate of fifty-two per minute, so that each turn of the four blades was driving us about fifty feet further from old England's shores. Albeit things were not as they should be (and would be presently) with our machinery department, and the information that six boiler-makers and thirteen engineers were working overtime below, threw some light on the more than usually pervading noises that from time to time emanated from the cavernous regions of the mighty engines.

A mystery that had presented itself to us on the landing-stage at Liverpool was now unravelled. Kind friends who were seeing us off were as green as ourselves as to the purpose of hundreds of folding chairs which were being embarked. No seats are provided on deck and each practical voyager was provided with a lounge of his or her own. We being new to the route had to hire at a fancy figure. Nothing could be more delightful than reclining in a spot sheltered from the wind, supplied with literature to taste from the well-stocked library in the saloon.

It was interesting to watch the steerage passengers, who mostly wore a happy and well-to-do aspect, and who now showed the contents of the bundles which each one had carried on board, and put to use the brand-new tins and kettles which had attracted our attention. Smart shawls adorned the heads and shoulders of the "gentler" sex (in many cases enveloping an infant of the "muling and puking" period) and potations of tea and something more potent were oftentimes partaken of from the hardware pots. There were cornets and accordians; and some of the people had good voices, singing sweetly in parts such melodies as "Sweet Belle Mahone." Among the men games of chance were very popular, and the wonderful "hands" that were turned up at Napoleon by fingerers of the dirty packs of cards were the amazement of our young gentlemen who knew the game. One player had the ace of trumps three times running, and then ace, king, queen, knave and ten—which of course got "nap." No fault was found, so it is to be presumed the game was genuine—and what interest could those characters have in swindling each other, and risk spoiling the pastime for the remainder of the voyage? We of the upper-deck were able to witness these lively doings by leaning over the rail, the lower-deck being so arranged that the less luxurious travellers had an open-air promenade the full length of each side of the ship.

DAY THREE.

Easter Sunday morning broke fresh and fine, with a fair breeze still from east-south-east, the course being west by south. The wind, increasing, gave rise to considerable motion of the vessel, which, at an early hour, placed several of our fellow-voyagers *hors de combat*. We spanked away at a fine rate, the sails being all set; not much of an assistance to a large steamer, but acting as a "steadyer," At ten a.m. the log showed that we were going sixteen and a half knots per hour, and at noon observations proved that our big floating hotel had gone over three hundred and ninety-five miles in the twenty-four hours. The course now set would take us about six hours south of the summer outward track, this detour being usual at this time of year in order to avoid the icebergs and fields of ice further north, which had been dangerously prevalent this Spring.

A Bishop, who was on board, administered Holy Communion at seven o'clock. He had on Saturday improvised an amateur choir, which had practised at the organ in the saloon. At half-past ten o'clock morning service was held in the Grand Saloon, at which most of the cabin passengers assembled, and such of the Protestants from the steerage who cared to avail themselves of the invitation to attend. The officiating Bishop preached an excellent sermon, and what we saw of him tended to improve our opinion of that dignitary of the Church—the Colonial Bishop. He was dutifully all there, "when refection bell did call," his daily walk amongst us keeping up that reputation which has been from time immemorial an attribute of his cloth, resulting in the popular conviction of all ages that finds expression in the line: "Who lives a good live is sure to live well." A newly-made acquaintance expressed pleasure at seeing a Roman Catholic priest taking a modest place and singing heartily at our Easter Matins. At one of his services in the steerage we attended, and were edified by the devotion and earnestness of the priest and his charge. Needless to say, our upper-crust congregation were conspicuous by their absence. I must say that Sunday was decently observed throughout the vessel. Members of the male sex, who often at home miss going to church, and when they do go do not deem it ***de rigueur*** to attire themselves in orthodox church-going garb, were here seen decorously clad in suits of broadcloth, and there were ladies ready with their favourite hymns when asked by the Bishop to name them, who perhaps had not had any favourite hymns, excepting those spelt h-i-m, for many years.

The number and variety of musical instruments in the ship was something extraordinary. From the organ and the grand piano in the drawing-room, to the concertina and bones on the lower deck, every noise-making machine that ever was invented appeared to be in constant operation. Some tunes and words which did not properly appertain to the Sabbath were heard occasionally, but "Moody and Sankey" predominated, varied by a kind of half-profane, half-treasonable, ditty by the Irish, the verses ending with such sentiments as these: "God save ould Oireland!" and "Oirelaind shall be free!"

The 1,400 steerage passengers were mostly English and Irish, the German and Scandinavian contingent of the week having gone by an extra Inman steamer, leaving Liverpool on the same-day. A detachment of the Salvation Army was amongst our lot, being sent over to join a previous company who were reported to be waging a victorious campaign amongst the benighted Yankees—a graceful return for the good worked in our islands by the two disinterested American evangelists who had twice come over to help us.

Harp, sacbut, psaltery, dulcimer, and all kinds of music were quickly hushed by a sudden shifting and freshening of the wind, which in an incredibly short space of time blew a stiff gale from the south-west, accompanied by a tremendous sea, calling forcibly to our minds the hymn of childhood:

When lo! a storm began to rise, The wind blew loud and strong; It blew the clouds across the skies, And roll'd the waves along!

The huge vessel behaved admirably, but about six o'clock the captain slowed the engines and slightly altered her course, head to wind, to lessen the heavy rolling. At this time the terrible Atlantic billows were making a clean breach over the ship, and everything that had not been made fast was either washed away or set careering about the decks in a manner which caused strange weird sounds to be heard in the cabins below, that were anything but reassuring. Whilst five of the crew were engaged in fixing the mast-head light, a sea, heavier than usual, struck the forecastle, throwing the whole of them down amongst the winches on the fore-deck. They had a narrow escape from going overboard, and the doctor, who was called away from dinner to attend to their injuries, reported that one had his ribs broken, another his kneecap broken and leg badly wounded, and the others less seriously hurt. This same wave dashed high over the pilot-bridge, far above the heads of the officers in charge, giving them a thorough drenching.

A dreary evening gave place to a bed-time fraught with gloom and dismal forebodings, but at midnight we were blessed with a slightly improved state of the weather, and in the small hours the engine were once more set away at full speed, the gyrations of the vessel and the accompanying noises continuing, however, to bar the possibility of any but the most fitful and unrefreshing slumbers.

DAY FOUR.

The next morning there was still a stiff breeze, now blowing from south-south-west, but the sea had considerably subsided.

Two more of our sailors had during the night been added to the five in the infirmary, but it was some satisfaction to learn that they were all doing well, and in no immediate danger, although it afterwards turned out that one of them was crippled for life.

It was surprising and pleasing to see the large proportion of passengers that turned up looking fresh and well to an early breakfast, and to hear that those who did not put in an appearance were enjoying fair health and petits déjeûners in the sanctity of their state-rooms.

The forenoon haul of the log gave a speed of fourteen and a half knots, and at noon our day's progress was noted as two hundred and eighteen miles only, so that our chance (if ever it existed) of making the quickest passage on record was "dished" for this journey.

DAY FIVE.

A change of wind; now blowing fresh from the north with bright sunshine, and smooth sea. The fair day's run of three hundred and forty-six miles was posted up.

In the early morning we passed a Cunard boat, bound from Boston to Liverpool, and overhauled a little French barque which run up the tricolour and saluted us by dipping it three times, a courtesy to which our British ensign duly replied.

An amusing story was told in the smoking room after breakfast. The emigrants from the Distressful Country, although provided for in a manner that might almost be termed luxurious, were frequently giving vent to that habit of grumbling, without the exercise of which existence would seem to be intolerable to them. A huge loaf of bread, about six times the size of an ordinary penny roll, was served to each man, woman, and child every morning, and no stint was placed upon them if they choose to ask for more, after consuming the first dole. One man, travelling by an Inman liner, requested to see the captain, and upon being shown on to the quarter-deck, had laid forth his grievance, which was that the breakfast allowance of bread was insufficient. The captain called for one of the rolls, and asked the complainant if that was not enough for any man's meal. Pat replied "I could eat half-a-dozen of 'em." "Then, by Jove," said the captain, "you shall!" and ordering up other five the Irishman was cured from future careless grumbling by having to exercise his powers of mastication and deglutition to a painful degree, and to experience a distension of the diaphragm the reverse of pleasant. It is but fair to state that he was allowed a drop of "the craythur" to wash down his unexpected repast.

Our good skipper, Captain Kennedy, had been upwards of four hundred times across "the pond," and was considered one of the ablest navigators of the age, having had command of the **Great Eastern,** and been twice employed in that capacity by the Government when she was under charter to them.

DAY SIX.

The course was now shaped in a more southerly direction, or about west-south-west, and there being a moderate wind from north-west a considerable rolling was experienced. Although cloudy, rain kept off, but a lowering temperature caused overcoats and wraps to be brought into requisition.

I paid my first visit to the barber's shop. The ***perruquier*** was a negro, who had his particolored pole protruded over his door on the main-deck. This worthy must either have paid a high rent or have been making a handsome thing of it, for his charge for shaving a saloon passenger was two shillings, or he would contract for a daily scrape during the voyage, long or short, for twelve shillings! This was the dearest piece of ***barberism*** I had had experience of. It beat a case in Paris where I paid eight francs for hair-cutting, shampooing, and trimmings.

During the forenoon we passed a schooner going east and a barque bound west. They hoisted their distinguishing flags, so that upon our arrival at New York they would be reported as having been "spoken" and the latitude and longitude stated, and all concerned in their welfare would learn the particulars from the published reports.

In the evening I saw a gentleman as near coming to his death as he could be without being killed. Instead of taking the convenient staircase leading direct from the smoking-room to our berths we preferred a breath of fresh air, and walked along the weather side of the upper deck towards the saloon companion. We found the door closed (on account of the spray the lee-door only had been left open), and my friend remarked "We have got to the wrong door," and before I could stop him turned the handle of the next door and stepped in. He was instantly out again with his hand to his forehead, gasping, "Oh, my God, what a sight!" I concluded that he had seen the effects of some horrible accident or suicide. When he recovered his self-possession he led me to view the cause of his perturbation. A narrow iron shelf within, upon which he had placed his foot, was all that had kept him from being precipitated to the bottom of the ship! Another step, which in the darkness he had partially made, and all would have been over. Needless to say that a remedy was at once applied to an oversight that allowed a doorway adjacent to the saloon entrance to remain on the latch as a trap to almost certain destruction. The brass handle was taken off and the iron door (which in reality was only intended for use in case of repairs) was barred up.

DAY SEVEN.

Having proceeded as far to the southward as was necessary, the vessel's head now pointed direct to New York, and with a gentle southerly breeze we slipped through the water at the splendid rate of sixteen and a half knots an hour. A slight stoppage during the night, however, doomed to disappointment the anticipation of a very big twenty-four hours progress. An increase in the number of revolutions of the propeller to fifty-four per minute, and there being so much less weight to drive through the water owing to the quantity of coal that had been consumed, still led to a high estimate of the run. Curiosity was set at rest by the announcement of three hundred and fifty-two miles. With a smooth oily sea we experienced our first really rainy weather.

Steamers and sailing vessels of all sizes were now so frequently sighted that we ceased to take notice of their coming and going in all directions.

DAY EIGHT.

We witnessed boat drill this morning. Although it was fine weather, the celerity with which each boat's crew got their craft ready and swung out on the davits, gave some idea of the readiness with which it could be done in case of abandoning the ship. We had eyed these boats daily with mixed feelings. To see them with covers off and fully equipped with kegs of water, provisions, and blankets, was to some extent reassuring, but their constant readiness was a continual reminder that some day it might be necessary for us to trust ourselves to their frail protection.

During the storm the previous Sunday we had been struck with the seeming impossibility of launching a boat into such a sea, or of it being able to live for a moment in it; and yet we know that vessels have been quitted in very heavy weather, and that some of their boats have weathered tremendous storms.

The slender barks in which foolhardy adventurers have crossed the Atlantic must surely at times have been borne on the crests of such mighty mountains of water as we gazed upon, and yet they have come safely to land!

No description or painting has ever conveyed to my brain an adequate conception of the intense vitality of even a minor storm at sea. That Easter Sunday tempest seemed calculated to blow the very eyebrows off one's face. And yet the ship was not dismasted, nor lost a single spar or rope-yarn; and the little French barque we had seen had evidently weathered the storm without a stick or a cord being damaged!

In the evening we had a grand entertainment in the drawing-room in aid of the funds of the Liverpool Sailors' Orphan Institution. Some excellent vocal and instrumental music was discoursed, and a collection of over sixteen pounds was taken. The Sunday's collections for the same object had amounted to fifteen pounds, so that, altogether, the Institution did pretty well out of the voyage. The liberality of the passengers did not end here, for a subscription towards the wounded sailors on board realized fifteen pounds, in addition to a halfpenny subscription worthily initiated and responded to in the steerage.

DAY NINE.

The three hundred and eighty-seven miles accomplished up to noon left two hundred and eighteen miles to be traversed to Sandy Hook (eighteen miles from New York town).

At one o'clock we took a pilot on board from cutter number twenty-one. There was considerable interest attached to this number, and all eyes and glasses had been directed to catch the first glimpse of it on the sail of the pilot-boat. A sweepstakes had been got up amongst some of the passengers, the fortunate holder of "21" receiving the sum of £12. There was a good deal of innocent "speculation" during the voyage, nothing being too trifling to make a bet upon, or upon which to base a "sweep," the number of miles run each day being a favourite medium of negotiation.

Being near to the close of our passage across the Western Ocean, notes were compared as to the comforts experienced in crossing, and it was instructive to ascertain the impressions of those who had made many Atlantic voyages; and most of the people in the saloon had done so. Old stagers declared that, even at the risk of having to spend a day longer on the sea, they would prefer a passage in the *City of Rome* to crossing in any other vessel afloat. Certainly for our own part (and here reference to the diary of my wife bears me out) the most grateful feelings remain for the courteous attentions of the kind officers, the genial doctor, and the assiduous stewards and stewardesses on board. From the splendid system of electric lighting throughout the ship, to the pneumatic bells, affording communication between every apartment, nothing on shore could be more complete than the conveniences and modern luxuries of this latest noble addition to one of the great ocean fleets of the world.

DAY TEN.

At four o'clock in the morning we passed Sandy Hook, and arrived at the quarantine station about seven. It was truly splendid weather, and a bright sun shining through a crisp atmosphere gave a very cheery introduction to the New World. There was not a cloud or suspicion of haze to mar the brilliancy of the April morning.

The tender came alongside and took away the mails, and also our telegrams for the shore. An interesting sight was that heap of mail-bags brought up from the hold; tons and tons of them, labelled right through, "Liverpool to San Francisco," and so on.

We had for once to enter into intricate financial transactions on a Sunday morning, for it became necessary to change our English money into the almighty dollar and its aliquot parts and multiples. Much amusement as well as anxiety transpired over this business. One very cautious young man wrapped up his newly-acquired dirty bits of paper currency in cream-laid notepaper, with such endorsements as "This is a four-dollar bill, and I must reckon it equal to sixteen shillings," "Quarter dollar or twenty-five cents, say equal to a shilling." The fumbled worn-out greenbacks were a sorry exchange for our bright British sovereign, and reminded one of the currency disabilities of such countries as Russia and Italy, a scandal that the advancing prosperity of the United States will doubtless shortly cause to be overcome by the universal use of their handsome metallic medium.

I will not essay the pen pourtrayal of the glories of New York harbour, the aspect of Fort Hamilton, and the striking appearance of the great city with its suburbs of Brooklyn and New Jersey. The yet unfinished suspension bridge destined to connect the two first-mentioned was a graceful figure in the picture, which was enlivened by the constantly plying huge steam ferry boats.

The delay in the discharging and examination of our luggage was very distressing. It was nine o'clock when we stepped on shore, and having already had breakfast, we hoped soon to get to our quarters and thence to church; but it was noon before we were released, tired and vexed at the first experience of the "freedom" of these glorious States.

When will our boasted civilization so advance as to enable the world to do without those relics of the barbarous ages—Custom Houses! We were inclined to think that the rigid examination was all a farce, and only useful inasmuch as it gave an army of officers a pretext for drawing their salaries; but the "searchers" showed their raison d'être this morning at any rate, for one gentleman had to pay three pounds for duty upon five hundred cigars which had already paid duty on importation from Havanna into England, and another was mulcted in the amount of seventeen pounds for a breechloader worth half the money, a sum which he preferred to pay rather than have the gun impounded, as he was bound on a shooting expedition north of Lake Winnipeg. Both of these payments, we were afterwards told, might have been avoided by a little contrivance. However, they serve to point the vexatious operation of protectionist imposts. The duties are not charged to foreigners only, for an American gentleman had to pay eleven pounds upon goods worth about five pounds in Europe.

The first impressions as we walked towards the street-cars—as the tramways are termed—were decidedly unfavourable. Crude telegraph poles disfigured every street, and were particularly hideous in their clustering at the corners; dingy lamp-posts that would have disgraced the smallest English town blessed with gasworks were stuck about at every conceivable angle; and pawn-brokers' balls hung significantly over shops, the rottenness of whose wooden façades was ill-concealed by daubings of red, blue, and green pigment. It was a strange sensation; the surroundings imbuing one with all the feelings of being in a foreign land, and the signboards being so incongruously English and homely. The carriage road was almost impassable for pedestrians, and the sidewalks (**Anglice,** footpaths) were simply execrable; pitfalls, dust, and dirt, everywhere.

As we became familiar with the better parts of the city these drawbacks were altered in degree only—some streets were better and some worse. Twice in "stages," as the omnibuses are called, were we stuck fast in holes in the streets and had to get out and walk.

The services of street-cars are excellent, their frequent running, and the good connexion of the different lines making street travelling very easy. The elevated railroad (although a great eyesore) over the tramways and pavements, supplies to some extent the relief to the traffic on the level afforded in London by the underground railway.

The absence (or rather infrequency) of marks denoting the names of the different thoroughfares is a source of inconvenience to a stranger, who is reduced to the necessity of interrogating the police, a body who, to say the least of it, are not so ready to bear with the inquisitiveness of travellers as are their brethren of the English metropolis.

The care bestowed by the inhabitants upon their personal attractions was evidenced by the numerous establishments for the sale of face-powder and enamels, and by the frequency of such announcements as "Madame So-and-so, *Finger nails beautified.*"

The Fifth Avenue Hotel we found pretty much what we expected: a magnificent mixture of splendour and coarseness. The marble unimpeachable; but the unmentionable result of the filthy national habit rendering it in places repulsive and slippery; the *cuisine* excellent, but the officials and waiters brusque, and even rude.

The want of the most ordinary politeness everywhere was most marked, but we soon became accustomed to it and came to the charitable conclusion that it is the want of time that drives the Yankees to omit such supererogatory words as "please" and "thank you," "sir" and "madam." There is no standing still; meals are bolted as though to-morrow were to be the Judgment Day; and all things are done in a flash-of-greased-lightning style that is at first very wearing. But human nature quickly adapts itself to circumstances, and before many hours were over we were hurrying along with the stream, and the biggest boor in the black country might be considered a perfect Beau Brummell compared with the bustling, bumptious Yahoos we were in danger of becoming in sympathy with our surroundings.

On this, our first evening upon the continent of the Western Hemisphere, we were fortunate enough to witness one of the most beautiful displays of the aurora borealis that has ever been recorded outside of the Arctic Circle.

DAY ELEVEN.

We drove through Central Park, a breathing-space in every way worthy of the Empire City which encircles it. Returning seaward we found Broadway not such a broad way as its name and reputation justified us in expecting. In width and length it is not unlike Oxford-street. Some of the buildings are much handsomer than the majority of those in the great London thoroughfare, and others are paltry and altogether unworthy of the vicinity. Flagstaffs adorn many of the edifices, and their huge banners, bearing in many instances the name of the owner of the emporium or "store," floated out upon the breeze. The wind blowing across the line of the street caused the bunting to spread nearly from roof to roof, which had a pleasing effect as the flags spread out against the background of blue sky.

Everything was very dear. The famous sign of "Delmonico's" struck our eye, and at a bar inferior to that of the Criterion or Gaiety at home a generous friend had to pay ninety cents for two thimblesful of brandy and a "split soda."

The charges at the hotels are large, but not out of the way if the "guest," as he is designated, partakes fully of all the meats to which he is entitled. But the full day has to be paid for, no matter how poor the appetite, or how many meals may be partaken of out of the house. The slightest item indulged in beyond the recognised service is rigidly charged for. For instance, if you are so confiding as to run the risk of theft by putting your shoes outside of your bedroom door to be cleaned, and you should be so fortunate as to get them back again, a charge of ten cents appears in your bill. That is, if you get a bill, a document which the mere asking-for brings down upon you the scornful and pitiful smile of the mercenaries of the cash-office.

The prices for hire of carriages are almost prohibitory to possessors of English incomes; two dollars from steamboat to hotel, and more than that from hotel to depot (railway station), being the very least if you have the luggage necessary for a moderate American tour. Ten shillings is extorted for a distance which a London cabby would blush to ask half-a-crown for. There is another mode of getting your baggage conveyed (the word luggage is unused in America) and that is by the "express," an institution which takes in hand your packages, giving you a brass "check" for each, in exchange for which you recover your belongings at the baggage-office at the depot. This system is absolutely necessary if your "pieces" are very large and numerous, but the cost of equal to a shilling for each article makes it come as expensive as taking the "hack" (never called a cab.) In the matter of expedition the waggons of the baggage express do their work in a fairly satisfactory manner, generally arriving at the desired point as quickly as yourselves; but in some cases of *arrival* we found the delays vexatious, having had to wait for more than an hour before the longed-for toilet, after a lengthy journey, could be accomplished.

I had a look into the Hoffman House Hotel, which boasts the finest drinking-bar in the world, where the proprietor (the notorious Fiske, who got off so easily with a brief incarceration for shooting Mr. Seward on the staircase of the Fifth Avenue Hotel), had recently paid two thousand pounds for a handsome oil painting, the subject of which was so "classic" that I dare not describe it here. No expense had been spared to make the place attractive; not only splendour, but chasteness and quiet elegance being everywhere evident in the "fixings."

Most of the waiters at the hotels and the porters and guards of the rail roads (two words, "R. R." for short, and never railways) were Irish, or of Irish descent, the brogue of the latter being as marked wherever we went as that of the latest Hibernian arrival. Upon the whole their want of civility was made up for by their smartness and intelligence.

The gentle aspiration of the first syllable of "hotel" is one of the few improvements which our language has sustained by acclimatization across the Atlantic; it has been rendered really a pretty sounding word as compared with a rendering of it obtaining in some parts of Britain.

The vestibules of these palatial buildings are crowded by sitting and moving groups of male persons in an everlasting buzz of conversation, or "chewing" or smoking for ever. We cogitated as to whether these were all guests and their callers, and as to the social status of the wearers of the shiny hats and respectable attire. Our perplexity was removed, as to at least one of these loungers, when we saw an immense swell with an extra polish on his boots, an extra curl to his moustache, and puffing away at a fragrant Havanna. The face was familiar; where had we seen it? It was Dick, the smoke-room steward of our ship! Only two nights ago we had sent the hat round and presented poor hard-working unshaven Richard with a nice little sum, and to-day he rubs shoulders with us, his distingué air commanding more attention from the minions of the establishment than do the passengers who but yesterday were waited upon by the fellow-guest of to-day.

In Madison Square is a gigantic bronze representation of a female hand and arm, holding a brazen torch. This singular erection is protected around the elbow, where it emerges from the earth, by a châlet of wood. The arm is large enough to contain a spiral staircase, which will one day be placed within it, for this work of art is part of a lighthouse in course of formation for Rhode Island, where it will stand in the novel form of a huge statue of Liberty, the home of the lighthouse-keepers being in the body of the figure instead of in the ordinary prosaic pillar of a light-tower, and the lantern will be held aloft by the colossal hand, in place of the bronze presentment of flame now issuing from the torch. This noble work is a graceful present to Columbia from her sister republic of Gaul.

At four o'clock in the afternoon we "went on board the cars" (we are now getting into the way of using a few of the more indispensable Americanisms) at Forty-second Street Depot, the terminus of the New York Central Railroad, *en route* for Boston. All the cars are of one class, excepting that you can have a seat in a parlour car by paying, in this case, a dollar extra. We tried the ordinary carriage on this occasion and found our first railway travelling in America very satisfactory, the fare being lower for the distance than at home, and the speed and comfort at least as good. We did the two hundred and thirty-six miles in six and a half hours, without changing seats.

It may not be out of place to give a description of the car, for, although the details may be familiar to many readers, still it is possible that many such little matters are often left undescribed, on account of writers and verbal narrators deeming them top well-known to need telling about. An instance of the desirability of minute description is at hand in the wrong impression conveyed of transatlantic railways by the stage adaptation of Jules Verne's "Round the World in Eighty Days," which shows an attack of Indians upon a train, the engine of which is American, but the vehicles, *English* railway carriages of various "classes," instead of the proper long "silver palace" cars, and passenger, baggage, mail and express cars of the country. The car is entered from each end, and has an aisle down the centre, on either side of which is a score of seats, each holding two persons. The velvet-cushioned backs of the seats are reversible, but most of the passengers sit facing the engine. If your party should be three or four, it is very convenient to be able to "fix" the "section" so as to travel vis-á-vis; on the other hand, if there are only two of you, there is quite as much privacy as in the Old World compartment system, and at the same time the convenience of being able to walk up and down the whole length of the train. Every car is fitted with a stove, from which pipes are carried under all the seats. This arrangement, together with the double windows (which it is treason to open), renders the atmosphere uncomfortably warm, as is the case in all the rooms and apartments. A boy goes round every few minutes with a tin of iced water and glasses, each passenger partaking as he fancies.

The sallow complexions of the people being as common to them as their habits of hurried eating, breathing stifling air, and imbibing cold liquids, it is possible that these may stand in the relation of effect and causes.

The aspect of the district passed through was novel and interesting, a surprising feature being the yet utter absence of foliage from the trees, as before we left England the leaves there were fully out. The advertising enterprise of the go-ahead inhabitants has caused landscapes to be blurred by huge letters being painted upon rocks and trees, such inscriptions as "Try Blair's Cough Mixture: it never fails," being found alike by railway side, on tops of mountains, and at bottoms of valleys.

A monstre hoarding erected well within sight of the line recorded that "Exactly twelve miles from this spot stands the Emporium of the celebrated St. Jacob's Oil, at 999, Broadway, New York." This oil, "Sozodont," and a certain stove polish kept us company throughout the entire continent.

DAY TWELVE.

We broke fast betimes at our hotel, the Brunswick House, at Boston. The excellent negro waiters were quite a contrast to the New York attendants. The breakfast is a most important meal here, and is partaken of with much zest. It commences at seven, and the early start gives an enhanced value to the day. Two or three oranges preface the repast, then a draught of the iced water which stands at your elbow throughout every meal. This is followed by oatmeal mush (porridge), hominy, cracked wheat, buckwheat cakes, an immense choice of boiled, fried, and broiled fish and flesh, vegetables in every form, and eggs—the latter prepared in a variety of ways, described in the *menu* as "broiled, dropped, fried, scrambled; and omelets, plain, with onions, parsley, cheese, ham, kidneys, or jelly." Plain boiled eggs are not eaten direct from the shell, but three or four are broken by the waiter into a tumbler, and stirring the yolks and whites together, with pepper, salt, &c. to taste, you then proceed in the usual manner with a spoon.

Thus fortified, we sallied forth to "do" the city of Boston, a delightful task, the associations connected with the place, and its splendid, clean, wide thoroughfares, making it peculiarly interesting and enjoyable. It is the Edinburgh of the States. Bookshops abound, and by far a larger quantity of books are sold in proportion to population than in any other American city.

Harvard University is at Cambridge, three miles out, and we readily reached it by the tramway, and went through the spacious grounds and buildings, including a magnificent memorial hall erected to the memory of students who fell in the Civil War; Saunders Theatre, &c.

Immense enterprise is being shown in developing the harbour of Boston and adding to its numerous docks, the New York and Erie Railroad Company having just completed a handsome dock, grain elevator, and warehouses, where four of the largest ocean steamers can be loaded or discharged at one time with a minimum of twenty-three feet depth of water at low tide. The "freight cars," or goods trucks, come right across country from the far West, and we saw some laden with provisions, such as bacon, lard, &c., that had come over two thousand miles. When we were informed that only a fraction over twenty per cent of the available producing ground of the great continent had yet been cultivated, the future of the exporting cities, as railways every month penetrated farther afield, appeared to be illimitable. We afterwards had ample opportunity of forming our own estimate of the productiveness of much of the "virgin" land forming the estimated four-fifths that our Boston friends relied upon; and also saw and heard much *of worn-out* soil, which a quarter of a century of incessant "cropping" had rendered as expensive to cultivate as farms in the British Islands.

The pride which the Bostonians justly take in their city is shown by their lavish expenditure upon the public buildings, such edifices as the post office and custom house being perfect masterpieces of architecture. The latter is surrounded by granite columns, each in one piece of forty tons weight.

We ascended by the "elevator," as the lift or hoist is invariably termed (an indispensable adjunct to every American building of any pretensions) to the roof of the palatial offices of the Equitable Insurance Association, and obtained from a height of a hundred and eighty feet a complete panorama of the place; the monument on Bunker's Hill, and that on the Common to the citizens who fell in the war with the South, being conspicuous.

The electric light and telephone we found in much more general use than at home; in fact a merchant told us that without the telephone it would now be impossible to carry on the business of the day. Not only for the immediate neighbourhood is it "laid on" but the voices of communicators are discernible giving orders for goods from villages forty miles away.

Instancing the intellectual tastes of the people I may mention the proprietor of a telescope of two hundred diameters, who, in the open street, drove a roaring trade by exhibiting the spots on the sun by day, and the planet Jupiter in the evening.

DAY THIRTEEN.

We proceeded to Albany *via* the celebrated Hoosic tunnel route: two hundred miles in seven hours. The tunnel itself is four and three quarters miles in length, the longest in the world after those of Mont Cenis and St. Gothard—so the Americans say.

At Greenfield station I applied at the refreshment stall for a glass of beer, but the proprietor said that he was not allowed to dispense intoxicants, and that it was with difficulty that he could get the authorities to let him sell cigars! This was a new phase to us of American affairs. A glass of cold rich milk, however, proved an excellent substitute for the coveted "laager."

The Delavan Hotel at Albany proved to be of the traditional Brother Jonathan type, and was just the hotel that descriptions in books had led as to expect to find. Frequently among the labyrinth of corridors a note appeared with an index finger directing "to the fire-escape." Prompted by curiosity, and possibly by some idea that it might be useful to know the way, we traced out the route until we came to a *locked* door, so that had the house been in flames we should probably have had more experience of the "fire" than of the "escape."

On the highest point in the city stands the new Capitol, a splendid building of Maine granite, in the style of the Renaissance—the handsomest and largest edifice in the States, next to the Federal Capitol at Washington.

The only one of fifty-four churches we visited was the Cathedral of the Immaculate Conception, and we were much impressed with its Old World appearance, which it owes to the rich stained-glass windows, shedding their "dim religious light" upon the vast space capable of accommodating over four thousand worshippers.

DAY FOURTEEN.

Embarking on board one of the magnificent Hudson river steamboats we quickly passed down stream, through the pretty but somewhat monotonous scenery, as far as the town of Hudson. After that the panorama was quite equal to the scenery of the Rhine, and in one part almost as grand as the Iron Gate of the Danube. This is saying a very great deal, but it is the honest opinion of one by no means prejudiced in favour of anything American, and who has traversed the course of all three rivers under circumstances favourable for comparing them. The romantic associations of the grand German river are wanting in the New World stream, but points upon the banks of the latter are rich in memories of thrilling interest, and the absence of "ruins" and little hovels of "castles" is rather in its favour than otherwise.

In the evening in New York I looked into one of the billiard halls of the country. It was well lighted and ventilated, and filled with an orderly company. There were eighteen tables, chiefly without pockets, upon which was being played the "canon" game with four huge balls and ponderous cues. A few of the tables had six pockets, the pockets being much larger and the tables much smaller than English ones. These were used exclusively for "pyramids" and the game was very quickly over. The charge was ten cents per game, and for billiards by time one cent per minute. A novel and useful mode of counting was in vogue which might be adopted with much convenience where a marker is not always available. A brass wire suspended lengthways above the table had strung upon it counters that were easily separable upon being touched with the side of the cue. One half of the string was devoted to white markers, the fifth and tenth being black of larger sizes; the other half being black discs with fifth and tenth of white.

The Fifth Avenue Hotel was so full of guests that beds were laid upon the floors of the drawing and reception rooms, so that we were fortunate in having rooms secured. Having occasion to procure a bottle of brandy to complete the equipment of our medical chest for our journey to the Far West, the price was six dollars—about five-and-twenty shillings—and we were consoled with the assurance that it was "the very best"; and so it ought to be, thought we.

DAY FIFTEEN.

We journeyed to Philadelphia by the Bound Brook route. The weather continued very cold, but bright. It was a strange coincidence that one year ago to-day we had occasion also to note unusual cold for the time of year, having then (21st April) experienced snow in Vienna.

We found the roadways of Philadelphia even more rugged and uneven than those of New York, there being huge holes in the middle of the best streets, and the crossings were very bad. The railways are all on the level, and the locomotives with their great clanging bells in place of whistles, are mixed up with the "street cars" and "stages." The trams were all drawn by horses or mules, and none of them had seats on the top, as at Hamburg and other European cities, where a fine view of the neighbourhood can be taken at a small cost by riding to the various suburbs upon a steam or horse-drawn car.

We continued to notice the plain, good English spoken, particularly by the negro population. There was very little of the expected nasal twang, which we began to suspect was more affected by the citizens of the U-nited States when in Eu-rope than at home.

DAY SIXTEEN.

We had a splendidly clear day for inspecting the largest city in area in the country, and second in population, there being nearly a million inhabitants. Brook Street is twenty-three miles long, and it and Market Street are fine thoroughfares, but the other streets are poor, and have all the objectionable points of American cities—open drains, filthy and rotten wooden shades over the footpaths, rough telegraph posts, &c.

The houses on the streets running east to west are numbered one hundred to two hundred, and all between Second and Third Streets two hundred to three hundred, and so on; so that the number of the house indicates the number of the street as well. Thus number eight hundred and thirty-six is in (or "on" as the Americans say) Eighth Street, and you know that you are sixty-four houses off Ninth Street. This plan is very convenient in going about, as whenever a number of a house can be seen the distance from the river Delaware or any desired locality can be calculated and its direction determined.

After visiting the shipping we took a carriage and drove to and through Fair-mount Park, the largest city park in the world, lying for fourteen miles on both sides of the river Schuylkill which is crossed by elegant bridges. The Laurel Hill Cemetery extends along the crags overhanging the river, and, with its white marble obelisks and mausoleums, interspersed with dark cypresses and rocky peaks, is singularly picturesque.

The houses in the suburbs will vie with any European city, the Pensylvanian marble which is so freely used in their doorsteps and façades giving them a handsome substantiality and richness of appearance.

The Centennial Exhibition building of 1876 was yet only partly pulled down, and what was left standing gave a fair idea of its vastness and splendour. The Memorial Museum in connexion with it is a fine marble structure, and was yet but partially furnished with articles of art and *vertu.*

We went through another solid marble building, after the pattern of the Madelaine at Paris, the Girard Hospital. This is a foundation that has multiplied its value, owing to the once suburban lands with which it was endowed by one Merchant Girard, having become part of the city. Its usefulness in providing education for fatherless children is thus tremendously extended.

We left Philadelphia from the Broad Street Depot, a new railway station that was the finest we had yet seen in the States. A gigantic railway map, painted on all one side of the large waiting hall, was at once the most singular, and the most useful adjunct to a railway station that had yet been conceived. The idea was probably borrowed from the huge map of France, which occupied a wall of the Paris Exhibition. As a rule the railway stations were the veriest hovels, mere sheds, out of all keeping with the sumptuous carriages and grand hotels of the country.

DAY SEVENTEEN.

On Sunday morning at Washington we experienced a tremendous snowstorm. The splendid auroras seen lately, the spots on the sun, the electric disturbances, and the icebergs in the Atlantic, had at last culminated in a heavy visitation of late winter in this part of the New World of the same latitude as Madrid.

Some of the trees in the streets and avenues of this City of Magnificent Distances were just in the opening beauty of their delicate green leaves, and these, bearing their weight of fleecy snowflakes, afforded a strange spectacle. The remainder of the trees, being yet unleaved, presented, together with the snow-covered houses and streets, an ordinary winter picture. The asphalted pavements of the fine broad thorough-fares were almost impracticable for horses, whose feet obtained little holding through the feathery carpeting of white. We, however, managed to get driven at walking pace to the Episcopal Church of the Ascension. The service was "low church," the responses being "said" in voices at various pitches; and the hymns, Te Deum, and canticles being sung (mostly as solos) by fine voiced young women and half a dozen male persons, perched up beside a fair organ in a gallery behind us. The service was almost identical with that of our own Church of England—President and Congress being substituted for Queen and Parliament in the prayers for each. The Nicene Creed was placed after that of the Apostles, the "ordinary" having the option of using either; and at the end of the ten Old Testament Commandments, came the New Commandment and the second like unto it, prefaced by the words, "Hear also what our Lord Jesus Christ saith."

During the singing the people sat or stood as they thought fit, fully one-fourth of the congregation remaining sitting. All sat while the sentences were being read and the collection taken. At various times there were arrivals and departures, particularly during the hymn preceding the sermon.

In the evening we again sallied forth in search of a place of worship, and presently came to a building of ecclesiastical appearance. We were told by an interesting little girl at the door that it was a "collared Baptist" Church. Now, we had known Baptists of various kinds, but had never had them "collared" before. It turned out to be a sanctuary for *coloured* worshippers. The negroes have their separate churches and chapels. A black minister was officiating, the whole black congregation constituting the choir, and sweetly they sang familiar hymns to the grand old psalm tunes of home. Our presence did not seem to be relished, so we departed and found close by, the Church of the Holy Cross.

Here we found an American example of Ritualism. After the bald service of the morning there was a difficulty in bringing the mind into proper frame for this florid celebration of evensong. There was an incongruity about the hard-headed Yankees taking to such a service. Being untrammelled by any State Church laws, the priest did just what he liked. The performance would, however, compare favourably with similar ones in England, and the surpliced choir and organist executed their part of it well.

Returning to the Metropolitan Hotel by Pennsylvania Avenue, the moon shone brightly upon the dazzling snow. The Capitol, always white, now stood out against the sky a magnificent object, its dome and roofs mantled with pure snow and bathed in the soft lunar sheen.

The **Washington Post** of the following day said: "The storm yesterday, coming as it did but a few days before the opening of May, proved too much for the recollections of even the oldest inhabitants. There have been one or two previous snows in the present generation as late in the Spring, but none so violent and wintry as that of yesterday. Fortunately for the fruit trees, it was confined to a very small area. It broke down telegraph wires, broke branches off trees, blocked up travel to some extent, and did considerable damage of a trifling, but annoying character. The snow-storm of the 23rd of April, 1882, will long be remembered."

DAY EIGHTEEN.

We made a retrograde movement upon Baltimore, which seaport we had passed in the dark upon the road from Philadelphia. An hour's ride brought us into the heart of this busy city. Taking a steam launch we sailed down the commodious harbour, and visited first the splendid British steam-ship **York City,** which vessel had discharged a cargo of mineral from the Mediterranean. The two thousand five hundred tons which she brought had been taken out in two and a half days, proving the facilities of the port for that kind of work. Next we boarded the **Glenrath,** delivering a consignment of old iron railway plates and **potatoes** from England. The last-named importation showed that a variation on the relative harvests can cause a material alteration in the account for food stuffs between the old country and the new.

As instancing the price of labour in parts of Europe, as compared with the United States, may be mentioned the case of a cargo which we noticed coming from the steamship *Glenbervie.* It looked like iron stone, but was actually chrome ore for a manufactory of colours in Baltimore. There are mines in the immediate neighbourhood which ordinarily keep the works supplied, but it occasionally pays to give a freight of thirty shillings per ton and have the mineral brought from Macri, in Turkey, where it is carried across the mountains to the vessels on the backs of donkeys, each animal being led by a woman or child, also laden with a bag of the ore. By this crude method two thousand tons had been shipped into the *Glenbervie* in the comparatively short space of ten days!

The grain-exporting trade for which this terminus of the extensive Baltimore and Ohio railroad is eminently adapted was, at the date of our visit, at a standstill, the gigantic "elevators" being almost empty. We went over the newest one, with bins for nearly two millions of bushels. There is a larger one at Chicago, but this one comprehends more modern "fixings" for storing, sorting, cleaning, distributing and shipping the grain than any other in the world.

A staple industry of Baltimore is preserving oysters in tins. An inexhaustible supply of large and excellent bivalves is procured from the neighbouring Bay of the Chesapeake, and although they become out of season for local consumption, the "tinning" goes on all the year round. Possibly by the time they come to be eaten they have become in season. A peculiar sight was a a hill composed of hundreds of tons of oyster-shells which are disposed of to make roads, or burnt to make excellent lime.

Inspection of the City Hall and the usual edifices and monuments occupied the afternoon, and we took our departure for Washington not much impressed by the architecture of the somewhat ostentatiously termed City of Monuments. The title was doubtless acquired when the monuments were many and the houses few; now the city has increased tenfold and the statues and columns are comparatively scarce.

DAY NINETEEN.

The melted snow and succeeding genial sunshine caused all nature to rejoice in springtide glory. Every twig put forth its leaflet and the sward assumed its vernal hue and freshness. The denizens of the Atlantic States now reckoned themselves fairly launched into spring, and chilly days would rapidly give place to the warmth begotten of longer spells of hours betwixt sunrise and sunset.

Right gay was the city of Washington as we ascended the steps to the back door of the Capitol. For be it known that this pretentious erection turns its back upon the city, the sixtons statue of Liberty, which tops the dome,—cast at Munich—the principal façade, and the portico whence each new President is proclaimed, are at the further side of the building. This is explained by the fact that it was intended for the heart of the legislative metropolis to lie to the east of the Capitol, and for the White House, a mile and a half to the west, to be a retired residence for the President away in the suburbs. Very few houses have, however, been built to the eastward, the avenues laid out towards the west having been built upon in a spread-out fashion. Washington selected the site himself, and it was laid out according to his plan, but as the eighty intervening years have passed over with only a comparatively small amount of building going on—and that mostly where the outskirts were intended to be—the city covers a very large area for its population of only a hundred and fifty thousand. Hence its "Magnificent Distances" title.

The prospect from the balconies of the Capitol is an extensive and pleasing one, the absence of smoke, owing to the use of anthracite coal, allowing a clear view for many miles. The main thoroughfares, radiating as *boulevards* like the spokes of a wheel from this centre-point, betoken the conception of a model city. One division of the circle has been kept entirely in the possession of the nation, and within it are the national conservatories and other federal institutions. An ugly railway station had been recently protruded into this reserved portion, but it was evident at a glance that sooner or later it would have to be removed. Every American is proud of Washington, and they all cried out against this eyesore. An unfinished column, intended to be crowned by a colossal statue of the Great General, stood for away, over in the Mall; but work was suspended owing to lack of funds.

The Capitol is characteristic of the Americans for, immense sums of money having been spent upon it, they mar the whole thing by stinting a few dollars upon it at the finish. The lamp-posts which adorn (?) the steps and balconies would be put to shame by an ordinary gin-palace gas lamp; and in front of the building is a dirty pool of water containing a few hungry gold-fish, and surrounded by a rusty iron paling, where a handsome fountain would fitly have decorated the approach.

Both Senators and Representatives were sitting at the sensible hour of noon, it only being in cases of urgent business that the Houses are kept at work until evening (that is "evening" as we understand the term for the American evening commences at noon—an example among many that the language is there being changed, not always in the direction of improvement).

The two Houses of Congress conduct their business pretty much on the same lines. An annually elected Speaker presides in the Lower, and the vice-President of the Republic (as President of the Senate) in the Upper Chamber. The seats face the tribune in concentric half-circles, and the members ate not divided upon Government and Opposition benches, but each has his own comfortable arm-chair and desk. This causes much inattention, gentlemen engaging in their private correspondence instead of attending to what is going on. The tobacco-smoking indulged in by members who were promenading, and lounging on seats, behind a rail defining the floor of the House proper, was very objectionable. There are ample galleries round each chamber for visitors, and ladies and gentlemen promiscuously obtain admission with out any "orders."

Shortly after our entrance our British blood was made to boil by the deputy from New York, Mr Robinson, who reviewed briefly the facts relative to the imprisonment of American citizens abroad, and thought that in view of those facts it was apparent that the United States Government was getting careless of the honour of its flag and the rights of its citizens. Since the beginning of the Government it had not been fortunate in its representatives to the Court of Great Britain. With all due deference to Mr. Lowell, he declared that the American suspects were quite equal to him, and some his superior, and he had no right to look down from the throne of his superciliousness on those honest American citizens who had called on him for assistance. He thought that Mr Lowell ought to be recalled, and he had a resolution which he would offer. He also had it in his mind to introduce a bill entitled "A bill for the relief of England, for the benefit of Ireland, and for the glory of the United States." He was not going to let it out on this occasion, but he had the plan in his mind, and it ought to be carried out and an end put to all this trouble. In the course of his remarks he characterised Mr Gladstone as the "deliberate fraud of the nineteenth century," and contrasted the "former glory of England under her Johns, her

Henrys, and her Georges, with her present shame under her Gladstones, her Brights and her Forsters." It was asked what should be done if England refused to comply? "I say fight," continued Robinson; "Washington said, Independence or fight;' Madison said, 'Give up the right of search or fight,' and I say, and this House and all true Americans say, 'fight!'" (see **New York Herald,** April 26th, 1882). I presume that I must have infringed the regulation as to "silence in the galleries," as, at the polite request of an attendant, I forthwith "made traces," but quickly regained admittance at the other side in time to see the division taken. The Speaker announced "Those in favour of the motion proposed by the **gentleman** from New York (**re** the recall of Mr Lowell) will say 'Aye' the contrary 'No.' The Noes have it." The result being challenged, he continued "The Ayes will stand up," and, after counting, announced the number; "the Noes will stand up," the result being the same as before. The Robinsonites being still unsatisfied, the challenge now took the form of a motion that "the roll be called." This being carried by the standing-up process, the clerk proceeded to call the names of the two hundred and ninety-one members in alphabetical order, the answers "Aye" and "No" being distinctly and rapidly given and jotted down. The alphabet of those who had not replied was quickly gone through a second time, in order to minimise the advantage which Z would have over A by being able to rush in from other parts of the building after learning that the roll-call had commenced.

The processes occupied nearly as long as a division in our House of Commons, but did not require the promenading into the lobbies.

We heard on every hand regret expressed at the decadence of the House, owing to universal suffrage having placed the seats in the hands of men who pandered to the mob, the result being that the best men in the country kept aloof from politics. Truth to tell, the Representatives were a sorry-looking set, and stories were rife as to the great fortunes amassed during a few years' membership, owing to the extensive corruption prevailing. One gigantic piece of jobbery was-brought prominently under our notice. The expansive roadways of Washington—in many places one hundred and sixty feet wide, exclusive of broad side-walks—are covered with a sea of splendid asphalte which is said to have cost the nation its weight in dollars, owing to the high tenders accepted in consequence of the heavy backsheesh paid by the numerous contractors to members of Congress to secure their support.

Before quitting the Capitol we went into the Supreme Court, where the Justices were engaged in hearing an appeal case. It is the only court in the States where the judges wear gowns, and they have no other garb of office. A naturalised Frenchman was pleading, but neither he nor his brother counsel wore any wigs or robes. There are nine Justices of the Supreme Court, who, besides constituting the final Court of Appeal, try cases where one State is at variance with another.

Strolling into the waiting-room of the principal railway station we were shown a brass cross let into the floor at the spot where President Garfield fell when stricken by the assassin's bullet, and upon the wall immediately above it a marble tablet briefly setting forth the melancholy circumstance.

DAY TWENTY.

Taking a herdick (small one-horse 'bus named after the inventor) we drove to the White House at the further end of Pennsylvania Avenue. This, the presidential residence, is a substantial and elegant building, and the furniture of its noble apartments betokens neither stinginess on the part of the tax-payers, nor lack of taste on that of its successive occupants. Here, as in the other government buildings, are plentiful paintings depicting battles where the "Britisher" is getting pretty considerably wholloped, such as "The Battle of Lake Erie," "Capitulation of General Burgoyne," &c.

Close by the White House are the Treasury, and Government Offices which are plain solid buildings of granite. After strolling through the principal chambers (which are thrown open to the public with scarcely any restriction) we went to the navy yard, where, among other interesting objects, are a fish-breeding house and a naval museum and library. We also had the privilege of inspecting a gunboat which was to start at midnight to take President Arthur and friends down the river to a naval review on Chesapeake Bay.

Never will we forget the kindness and hospitality we experienced at this interesting and delightful city. Colonel May, who with his wife and daughter did everything to make our sojourn in it enjoyable, was a native of Louisiana; but, being of English parentage had retained the privileges of his British nationality. During the lamentable civil war he had been one of the few Southern planters who remained loyal to the Union, and many of his experiences during that unhappy time are recorded in a book of thrilling interest written by him— *The Earl of Mayfield.*

The delicate task of further personal allusion to this charming family is saved me by reference to the Washington *Sunday Herald* of July the 30th, 1882, in which appears the following paragraph:—

"An interesting social incident has recently occurred illustrative of the magnetic powers of Washington as directly compared with the gay and seductive capitals of Europe. Col. Thomas P. May, the well-known and distinguished author of *The Earl of Mayfield, A Prince of Breffny*, and other works, came to Washington about three months ago. The Colonel has been abroad for about one year, spending the greater portion of his time in England, where he has numerous family connections and associations, as is amply testified in *The Earl of Mayfield.* No confidences are here violated, since it has become an open secret that many of the incidents embodied in that popular book are founded on fact, and that under the name of Carew is actually recorded a history of the ancient May family, of which the present Lord Chief Justice of Ireland is a member, and Col. May is the head. He came to Washington for a short stay only, but was so pleased with its numerous attractions and rare prospects that he has purchased the elegant residence of Admiral Wyman on the corner of G and Twenty-first Streets, and intends to reside in Washington for the greater portion of his time. With Mrs May, Washington is a household word, for, although married to an Englishman, she is a native of the South. Her father was the Hon. Miles Taylor, who was for many years a prominent member of Congress from Louisiana. He resided in Washington during the greater portion of the year, his only daughter being his constant companion. We welcome this charming lady back to the society she formerly graced. Both she and her lovely daughter, just budding into womanhood, will be an immense addition to the social charms of the political and polite capital of the Union."

The last dozen words are essentially American—one for the Mays and two for Washington—conveying the assumed superiority of the city over other "metropolises" of the States, as does the opening sentence over the "seductive capitals of Europe." New York and Boston have claims to be considered the capitals, "political" and "polite" respectively, the true designation of Washington being—the legislative capital.

DAY TWENTY-ONE.

We left Washington for the west in the forenoon, taking parlour-car tickets for Cumberland and "sleeper" thence to Cincinnati for the night travelling. The sleeping-cars are only so converted at bed-time, the beds being deftly folded away in the roof of the carriage during the day.

A great source of inconvenience in travelling is what appeal's to a stranger to be the foolish arrangement of clocks. An attempt is made by every large place to use solar time, hence trains are made to run as nearly as possible to the time of the sun. In the forty hours' ride now commenced we had three "times"—Washington, Vincennes, and St. Louis. It became absolutely indispensable to carry with our watches a reconciliation card with little dials showing the hour at a dozen different places when noon at New York.

To show the absurdity to which the subdivision is carried—it is one hours' ride between Baltimore and Washington, and the clocks are three minutes different, so that the journey one way is apparently six minutes longer than the other. We heard it stated that business could be conveniently carried on if there were three standard times—say New York, St. Louis, and San Francisco. The only way to be certain of catching a train is always to be at the station very early, particularly if you have luggage. There is a great deal of delay about "checking" the latter, and there is needless time wasted at both ends; but the system is very safe. No encouragement is given to taking parcels in the cars with you, and care must be taken to have just so much impedimenta with you as you can conveniently carry, as there are no porters to transport you from platform to platform or from train to cab or "stage." I use the word "platform," but the boards from which you enter the cars are laid level with the ground. Travelling trunks must be strongly made, as the fellows who handle them are called "smashers," and well they earn their appellation.

The time-tables provided by each line contain, within a highly coloured wrapper, the times, distances, fares and altitudes on one side; and on the other a map showing the particular rail road and its connections. The latter is very useful; a trifling fault, when it is known, being that the company's own line, marked by a thick black band across the map, is invariably shown to be as nearly as possible as the crow flies, whereas competing routes appear to be more devious than they actually are.

Our road traversed for the first two hours a beautiful, cultivated country, and then succeeded wild and rugged regions, with short intervals of farm land, until dark. Leaving the broad and winding Potomac (the accent on the second o, long) at the delightfully situated Harper's Ferry, where the Shenandoah flows into it, we found ourselves passing up the ravine of "Elk Branch, which, at first narrow and tortuous, widens until it becomes the charming valley of Virginia. Further on, North Mountain is crossed by a long excavation, where we saw, level with the line, two seams of coal of one to three feet in thickness, illustrating markedly the geological formation of the district. A poor and sparsely peopled country brought us to the commencement of the ascent of the Alleghany Mountains. For seventeen miles the train, drawn by two powerful locomotives, pursued its serpentine and upward way, the most of the time on the brink of deep gullies, where, hundreds of feet beneath us, the swollen mountain torrents rushed along their rocky beds, fed every few yards by foaming cascades which dashed under or over our very cars as we sped along.

At the extreme summit of the range, two thousand eight hundred feet above the sea, we noticed the waters hesitate which way to flow, and then exhibit a tendency to run in our direction, until very quickly the little rills united into the impetuous stream which formed the upper waters of the Youghiogheny river. Descending by heavy cuttings, embankments, and tunnels, for twenty miles, we reached the end of this mountain section at Grafton, and were glad to seek rest for our strained eyes in the repose of our travelling couches.

DAY TWENTY-TWO.

We were up with the sun, and after toilet and ablutions (for which the car provided tolerable facilities) we arrived at Cincinnati for a two hours' stroll round the city, during which we saw and smelt quite sufficient of the capital of Ohio. Here, as elsewhere until now, mules outnumbered horses as beasts of draught, and strong noble animals they were. We entered a German Roman Catholic church, where work women with their baskets beside them were kneeling in morning prayer, and a humble coffin lay in lowly state before the High Altar with burning tapers around it, awaiting the obsequies which would doubtless take place within a few hours.

At eight o'clock once more "all aboard" bound westward, and we partook of a good breakfast cooked and served in the train. The following *menu* was distributed throughout the cars.

"As you journey through Life Live by the Way." BREAKFAST Now Ready, Served in first-class Style, PRICE 75 CENTS.

A DINING CAR
Is attached to this train. "Eat and be satisfied!"
PASSENGERS Will appreciate this new feature of "life on the Road."
BREAKFAST BILL OF FARE. English Breakfast Tea. French Coffee.
Chocolate.
Ice Milk. BREAD. French Loaf.

Boston Brown Bread.
Corn Breads. Hot Rolls. Dry, Dipped, Cream and Buttered Toast. BROILED. Tenderloin Steak, plain or with Mushrooms. Spring Chicken.
Mutton Chops.
Veal Cutlets. Sirloin Steak.

Sugar Cured Ham. GAME IN THEIR SEASON. OYSTERS IN THEIR SEASON. FRIED. Calf's Liver with Bacon.
Country Sausage.
Trout. EGGS. Fried.
Scrambled.
Boiled.
Omelets.
Plain. RELISHES. Radishes.
Chow Chow.

French Mustard. Worcestershire Sauce.

Currant Jelly. Mixed Pickles.

Horse Radish. Tomato Catsup.

Walnut Catsup. VEGETABLES. Stewed, Fried and Boiled Potatoes. FRUITS. Apples.

Oranges.

We began to realize that we could become reconciled to the ways of the natives if they would only *eschew* some of their practices and provide us with less stifling atmospheres; for there is a robust honesty about their Republicanism and Democracy that is very refreshing after the kid-gloved Liberalism often met with at home, which relies upon the "left wing" of the party to do battle in the cause of progress, and feels a sort of comforting assurance that the "Tory drag" will keep the coach from rushing headlong down the hill.

Jonathan has not yet asked for a king, and so has not laid himself open to the answer, "Ye know not what ye ask"; but, on the other hand, there are thinking men who aver that the demon of unrest, and desire of those who have not to plunder those who have, will soon be let loose here as in older countries. The well-to-do classes are getting very fond of anything that bears early date in the history of the Union, and the public prints teem with such words as "ancient" and "venerable" applied to matters not yet a hundred years old. Institutions are fast becoming old enough and rich enough for the ***intransigentes*** of the near future to disestablish and disendow, and it remains to be seen whether a constitution, of which universal suffrage and paid delegates are essential elements, will be better able to cope with the coming Evil than the military despotisms and constitutional monarchies of the Old World.

There are strange inconsistencies in the constitution and in the actions of the United States Government. Among the latter may be classed the interdict of Chinese immigration; and as an instance of the former may be cited the fact that, whereas every white or black male person over twenty-one years of age has a vote, no Chinaman, Indian, or female, has a voice in electing members of the House of Representatives, however much they may be paying to the taxes of the nation.

DAY TWENTY-THREE.

Before crossing the Mississippi to St. Louis, the town of East St. Louis has to be passed through—or rather over—much in the same manner as the town of Gateshead has to be before the high level bridge conveys the traveller from the south into Newcastle-upon-Tyne; in fact the big city on the western bank of the great American river is not unlike, at first sight, the "canny toon" in the north of England. A magnificent steel bridge spans the Mississippi here, twelve hundred miles from its mouth, as wide as the Thames at Gravesend. Two stone piers carry three spans of five hundred feet each, approached by viaducts, and, on the western shore, also by a tunnel under the higher part of the city. The trellised spans support the railway, and above is a roadway with tramways and footpaths. Both rail and road rise slightly to the centre, which gives a graceful finish to the structure. We had a fine view of the bridge from the deck of one of the leviathan river steamers, the *City of Vicksburg,* which we inspected thoroughly. This floating palace of seventeen hundred tons burthen was by no means the largest on the river. Her draught loaded was only nine feet, but she often had to be lightened to get over the shoals when the water was low. Her space for stowing cargo was admirably adapted; and the large saloon, in white and gold, was, like all her arrangements for the comfort and convenience of passengers, superb and luxurious. She plied between St. Louis and Vicksburg, making the return passage in a fortnight, eight hundred miles each way; the many stoppages to deliver and receive cargo in going down about equalizing the time to the slower voyage against the stream in steaming back.

A drive to the Lafayette Park resulted in an enjoyable afternoon, the land and water being laid out with more than usual eye to sylvan effect. At length the trees had become fully clothed in green, that well set off the "brighter crimson" which, according to the Laureate, is given by amorous springtide to the "robin's breast;" and the "wanton lapwing" was exhibiting his "other crest" to decoy some feathery mate of that ilk to vernal nuptial bliss. The swans, storks, and other tamed birds, were occupied at their nests upon their several islets, safe from the disturbance of the transatlantic school-boy; and bands and fountains played, the latter making by far the more agreeable music this charming April day.

We left St. Louis with more regret than any other city of our tour, it having offered an agree able surprise—being in many respects the most satisfactory place we visited. The aspect of such a thriving port in the centre of a continent is unique.

The German population is very numerous and well-to-do, and keeps up its own language, churches, newspapers, and places of entertainment.

The Southern Hotel is not behind any in Europe for any one thing excepting situation; and for grandeur, size, and comfort combined, is not eclipsed on either continent. The Palace at San Francisco beats it for size, and the Windsor at Montreal for luxurious elegance; but the other three monstre hotels of the world—the Baldwin at San Francisco, and the Palmer House and Grand Pacific at Chicago, do not excel it in any material particular.

DAY TWENTY-FOUR.

We awoke amid the green wheat fields of Missouri, and the rich black soil where yet the coarse stubble of last year's corn crop was only partially succeeded by the new sowing which takes place in May for autumn reaping. (The term "corn" is applied exclusively to maize or Indian corn.) The wheat was thigh high, and expectations of garnering by the middle of June were indulged in. The rye was headed; and generally there were prospects of an early and abundant harvest.

Trim farmsteads—mostly of wood—appeared at long intervals; and, less frequently still, small prosperous-looking towns (beg pardon, cities) came into view. Broad rivers and miles of scrub and forest varied the landscape. Most of the cultivated patches were very rudely fenced and had the stumps of the felled trees of the primeval woods remaining as impediments to the working of the implements of the husbandman. The ever-moving panorama was alone worth the coming all the way from Europe to see.

Most of us are apt to stick to our old grooves, and if we can get somebody else to go over the seas and tell us about the other side, well and good; but we, we must go to Harrogate or Scar borough, where we can renew our acquaintance with the people we met there last year, and the year before, and the year before that, and make reservoirs of our stomachs for the nauseous waters of the place. We take a bath in the morning, walk to the station at train times, stroll up the town of an evening, go to bed and wish it was Sunday, for some of the people from home to come over and see us. And we call this going away for a change, and having a grand time!

Brunswick, on the Missouri river, had a special interest, as here a railroad crossed ours, forming the centre point of the elongated figure 8 which our track from Atlantic to Pacific and back was intended to (and ultimately did) describe. At Council Bluffs all passengers and baggage were changed into the cars of the Union Pacific Railroad, which was to take us a thousand and thirty-three miles to Ogden in two and a half days and two nights. Between Council Bluffs and Omaha (four miles) we crossed the Missouri river by a bridge three thousand yards long, and for the next twenty-four hours traversed the State of Nebraska.

DAY TWENTY-FIVE.

Our course lay along the north bank (or rather shore, for it was as flat as a pancake) of the River Platte, as far as Cheyenne, where we entered the territory of Wyoming, having seen spreading prairies for the first time in something like their vast nakedness and solitude. Settlements and farms there were; but, unlike those left behind us, they seemed to be swallowed up in the immensity of the boundless levels which rolled off to the horizon like the sea. For forty miles at one stretch was the railway as straight as if drawn by a ruler. Herds of antelope were feeding; and "villages," as they call them, of prairie-dogs broke the monotony of the plains.

We saw trains of emigrant waggons, bound Westward Ho, slowly drawn along by sturdy mules. These caravans were the straggling successors of the thousands of bullock-drawn waggons that wended in long trains up the course, of the Platte in pre-railroad days, sometimes for miles actually in the shallow water or dry part of the bed of the stream.

Scores of skeletons of oxen, and some in less advanced stages of decomposition (as many as a dozen could be counted in as many minutes), showed the small value of the carcases at this distance from populous places; neither skin, horns, nor hoofs being removed.

As an example of the mode of life up in these regions Cheyenne may be quoted. Its altitude is six thousand and forty-one feet, and population about as many souls as it is feet above the level of the sea. Endless and poor-looking prairies surround it, and it looks as though snow in winter and dust in summer would be its chief characteristics; and its ostensible sources of in come, supplying refreshments to travellers, and the carrying on of the waggon and locomotive shops connected with the railway. The guide books dignify it with the following description: "Schools and churches are as numerous as required, and society is more orderly and well-regulated than in many western places. It also boasts of a racecourse and some good 'steppers;' and (mark this, for six thousand people) two daily newspapers—the *Leader* and the *Sun.*" To show how these "cities" have been founded: "As lately as 1869 this place had her share of roughs, gambling-hells, dance-houses, and wild orgies; murders by night and by day were the rule rather than the exception. This lasted until the business men of the place tired of such doings, and a vigilance committee was formed which caused several of the most desperate characters to swing by a rope on some convenient elevation, and the others taking the hint quietly left the city."

Towards noon of this, the second day from Omaha, being bright and clear, we caught the first cloud-like sight of the snow-clad Rocky Mountains (I use the term snow-clad rather than snow-capped for we were already on an elevated plateau almost in the region of snow, so that the range of peaks which appeared was white to its visible base). Pike's Peak, a hundred and seventy-five miles off, was the first "mountain" which we saw. For thirty miles the train climbed up jagged granite rocks, winding in and out of the wooden sheds built to keep the snow off the track, in a manner to rivet all attention. These "snow-sheds" are very numerous and of all lengths, up to that of the most remarkable one, which is twenty-eight miles long! There are also fences—sometimes four deep—erected in places where eddies of wind have been proved to cause drifts which endangered the working of the line.

During the afternoon we reached Sherman, eight thousand two hundred and forty-two feet above the sea (about the same height as the site of the Hospice of St. Bernard), the highest railway station in the world.

The cold was severe when you put your nose out of the cosy, heated car: but the sensation was a new and delicious one, and must he a novel experience to any traveller, no matter how extended his previous journeyings may have been—for it is railway travelling still. This kind of progress is to be likened to a sea-voyage. One shakes oneself down, unpacks books and wraps in Pullman palace car, and pursues the ordinary occupations and amusements of home. Your meals are abundant, well-cooked and nerved, and not hurried. The speed at any time (out west) is not tiring, giving time to see well the curious and interesting sights with which the country through which you are passing abounds, and withal the air is singularly fresh and invigorating.

Instancing the frequency of the stoppages and the information afforded by the time-tables, the following is an extract from the U.P.R.R. Co.'s "folder."

West from Omaha.
Distance from Omaha.
Omaha Time.
Elevation.
East from California. Daily Emigrant
Daily Express.

Daily Express
Daily Emigrant P.M.
P.M.

P.M.

A.M. 5.20
3.43
549
Sherman

8,242

1.23

7.00 6.20
4.08
555
Tie Siding
7,985
1.00

6.25 6.50
4.25
558
Harvey

7,857
12.45

6.00 7.20
4.43
564
Red Buttes
7,336
12.30

5.35 8.05
5.10
570
Fort Sanders
7,163
12.12

4.57 8.20
5.20

573
Laramie

7,123
12.05

4.45

It will be noticed that for trains going westward, read downwards; for trains going east ward, read upwards.

DAY TWENTY-SIX.

During the night we passed over the second of the nine ridges of the Great Rocky Mountain region which we had to encounter, and at Creston were at the dividing chain of the western half of the Continent; the waters from the mountains here running in opposite directions—those to the east turning ultimately southward and entering the Gulf of California as the Colorado River, and those to the west emptying themselves finally into the Pacific Ocean from the Bay of San Francisco. Some writers assert that the eastward waters find their way into the Mississippi, but this has been refuted.

We passed a strange train that was shunted into a siding to allow us to pass, viz:—seventeen trucks of oysters, bound from the shores of the Atlantic to the Pacific Coast for "planting."

At Green River, where we breakfasted, were collieries in the desert, a valuable property of the Railway Company, supplying excellent coal for their engines, and enabling them to sell to the Central Pacific R. R. Co., and also to send to customers as far off as San Francisco.

The stoppages at the two hundred and fifty stations were lengthy, and the whole journey very leisurely, occupying six days and nights from ocean to ocean, whereas it could be done in four to four and a half. Doubtless the through traffic and that between the great centres is not sufficient to support a fast train each way daily, and so what is termed the "express" serves a local traffic which is no doubt remunerative, and also renders the travelling for through passengers more interesting and possibly less fatiguing than a mere flash across the Continent.

There was a car full of soldiers on our train going to assist in putting down the Indians who were "troublesome" Arizona, and as the Major who was with them told us it cost five white men to "quell" one Indian, there was some reason for the lack of martial glee among the braves bound upon this inglorious errand.

The table-land continued barren, and although the snow had here not all gone, and the ground was still moist with the melting of it, the warm sun had so far failed to cause any green grass to appear. We learnt that even in the most favoured parts of the continent very little greenness ever refreshes the eye, for the blazing heat of summer succeeds so rapidly upon the shooting up of the grasses, that all becomes brown in a very brief space of time. When such expressions as "rich pasturage" are used they must not be understood as indicating an *appearance* of richness, such as that of an Irish or even English meadow, but a nutritious self-made hay, of great value to the rearers of stock, hut not pretty to look upon.

In this elevated district it was difficult to imagine what the thousands of sheep could be eating, but near observation showed that there was a scanty brown herbage, between the bushes of sage-brush, that afforded them pasturage. Farther on we passed into a region of utter desolation, where the lack of moisture and the prevalence of alkali—which covered the face of the earth like dirty snow—debarred the possibility of any vegetation whatever, excepting the pertinacious and useless sagebrush—a poor-looking scentless shrub not unlike the fragrant plant from which it doubtless derives it name.

These deserts being part of the large proportion of uncultivated land which the Bostonians boasted of as yet to contribute to the prosperity of the export trade, our near acquaintance with them considerably improved our education as to American resources, commenced at the hands of our good New England friends.

Fellow-travellers belonging to the locality, who had tried all parts of the States in turn, said that crass ignorance prevailed in the East, and among members of Congress, as to the capabilities of the western states and territories; which, with the exception of parts of California and Texas, already supported as many people as could find subsistence. Glib talk as to irrigation from artesian wells in regions such as this was impracticable nonsense; the absence of rivers proving how little moisture was to be squeezed out of the rocks and gravelly formation. With a rainfall of only three inches per annum, as in Nevada, what could be expected as the result of attempts to grow cereals? Even the in habitants of Utah were compelled to leave their comfortably established territory to seek in numbers other grounds, their land having already more population than could be supported—chiefly through the want of water. The Government put too high a price upon land "out west." It would not pay anybody to buy it for cattle or sheep runs. To have to pay rates on it, it was not worth a cent an acre. The result was that men planted themselves down rent-free to rear cattle, and then sheep men would come and edge them off; and so a perpetual warfare was going on, culminating often in outrage and murder. This st

ate of things, said a shrewd settler, could be remedied by the Government giving up the expectation of selling lands for wheat-growing that would never do it, and granting reasonable leases of large tracts for cattle and sheep runs. This would result, as in Australia, in the land being taken up for its legitimate purpose, pasturage; and the lessees would arrange for the rearing and watering of their stock, as animals could travel to where the little water was, whereas crops could not, even if there was soil sufficient to grow them in.

To north and south we still carried with us the snowy peaks of the never-ending "Rockies," and admired their fantastic outlines against the perpetual blue of the sky.

At Evanston (just half way between the Missouri river and the ocean—nine hundred and fifty-seven miles from each) we first saw the Heathen Chinee in his numbers, the waiters at the refreshment room being Celestials; and we learnt that the adjacent coal mines, turning out two thousand tons daily, gave employment to eight hundred Chinamen.

The afternoon was spent in threading the Echo and Weber Canons (pronounced Canyons), the road winding through all their devious turnings, while rock-ribbed mountains rose to a fearful height to right and left. Emerging from these grim battlements of cliff, we entered Salt Lake Valley, and changing cars at Ogden, took a branch line to Salt Lake City, arriving there in time for supper, and early to bed.

DAY TWENTY-SEVEN.

At the Continental Hotel, we found in the visitors' book, "T. R. Richards, Special Correspondent, ***Tenant Farmers' Advocate,*** England." Doubtless Mr. R. was having a fine time of it around here "collecting information." Another, more important, entry in the book was the arrival that day of General Sherman, Commander-in-Chief of the army of the United States, accompanied by his daughter, General Poe, and Major Morrow, aide-de-camp. They had been through Texas, New Mexico, Arizona, and California. The General said that the army knew nothing about Indian matters until hostilities occurred and then it was powerless to do much, because the Indians got out of the way by the time the troops were notified and ready for action. He favoured the entire management of Indian affairs being placed in the hands of the army.

The Mormon capital is well laid out. There are two hundred and sixty blocks, each one-eighth of a mile square, sub-divided into eight lots, each containing an acre and a half. Trees and running water line each street, and almost every lot has an orchard of pear, plum, peachy and apple trees. The houses are. mostly of one storey, with separate entrances where the proprietor has more than one wife. To the north the mountains are close up to the city, while to the south are a hundred miles of plains, beyond which rise, clear cut and grand, the grey range whose peaks are covered with perpetual snow. The mountains immediately around the place are also almost always snow-capped, so that the hot and dusty valley is very much relieved by the sight of encompassing walls of white, and by the supply of irrigation water therefrom. It is a beautiful site for a thriving city, and is surrounded by a country rare in the elements of wealth, could the people all work for a common end. But the continual resistance of the stand still Mormons to the go-ahead Gentiles is keeping the place behind. There are still eighteen thousand followers of the Prophet out of a total population of twenty-one thousand, but at last the United States Government are taking steps to remove this blot of polygamy from the territory, and if President Taylor, the present head of the Church, is wise in time he will receive a "revelation" and declare to his people that no more plural marriages will be solemnized.

We were informed that there was not an honest Mormon, man or woman, who did not feel polygamy a disgrace and a shame. The proof was found in the actions of plural wives and their children. Whenever a second, third or fourth wife could, she passed off as the first wife, and their children claimed, whenever possible, to be the offspring of the real, the first, wife.

The electric light and telephone were in full swing here, there being between two and three hundred subscribers connected with each other by the Telephonic Exchange in this far-away community, and new electric light works were projected in competition with those already supplying the city with illumination.

The Tabernacle came on for early inspection. An erection whose highest inside elevation is sixty feet, and covered by an elongated dome possessing the acoustic properties of a huge whispering gallery. At its farther end, two hundred and fifty feet from the speaker, we could hear the faintest whisper, and a pin dropped into a hat caused rather more sound to reach us than if we had been close beside it. Upon asking the janitor if the effect was interfered with when the full seated congregation of twelve thousand persons were present, he replied, "Not at all, excepting by the noises the people themselves make; that which makes it good makes it bad, for every cough and rustling of dress is as distinctly heard as the preacher's voice."

Twenty large doors, opening outwards, afford exit for the vast assemblage of worshippers in a minute and a half.

The attendant had an unmistakeble Tyne-side accent, and he admitted to New-castle birth, and an ardent belief in Mormonism.

Whilst engaged at the entrance-lodge in choosing some photographs, I over-heard the following interesting colloquy between one of our party and the hoary-headed fellow-sinner in charge.

Our Party—"I hear by your accent you are a Scotchman."

H.H.F.S. (his manners evidently not improved by residence in Zion)—"I would rather be a Scotchman than an Englishman, anyhow."

"How long have you been a Mormon?"

"I preached in Scotland for thirty-three years, and have been here four years. Every man must be a preacher or he cannot go to heaven. That is, he must make known that which is revealed to him."

"Do you believe in Jesus Christ?"

"We are the only people who do properly."

"But He had no wives."

"How do you know that?"

"It is not in the Bible."

"Many things are true that are not in the Bible, so long as they are not contradictory to it. God has made revelations to His people in all ages. Jesus could not have gone back to His Father unless He had had three wives."

"How is that?"

"Because three is the quorum; so it has been revealed in these latter days."

"But how about us, who also believe the Bible, and do *not* hold with polygamy?"

"God is merciful, and if you have not had revelations to the contrary you may be saved."

There was no getting over this and we were fain to leave the old man in his paradise of security. Who shall say that his ardent faith will not be accounted unto him for righteousness?

Being told by this worthy that it was the correct thing for all tourists to pay their respects to "the President," we made for his residence, and sent in our pasteboard. A splendid mansion, truly, equalled only by that hard-by, erewhile inhabited by the Prophet, Brigham Young. Intending to have it out with this High Priest Taylor as to how he reconciled his conscience with this sort of thing and so forth, we were quite disarmed on be holding the benignant old gentleman who shook us heartily by the hand and bade us welcome to Utah. Surely anything that *he* believed *must* be right, and we had to content ourselves with congratulating him upon the growth of his community, hoping his wives were well, and bidding him good day. He vouchsafed the information that he was an Englishman, and had been thirty-five years at Zion, having come with the first saints who set foot amongst the Indians, who had always behaved well in return for the kindly treatment accorded to them. The Indians, he said, were very badly used in the parts where they made reprisals.

We here saw our first Indians, who looked orderly and happy enough, and having visited the never-to-be-completed Temple, and other institutions connected with the languishing creed, we pursued our way back to Ogden, where we took the

Central Pacific Railroad for our eight hundred and thirty-three miles ride to San Francisco.

Having sent home by post some of the fore going account of our visit to the Mormon metropolis for insertion in a provincial newspaper, the following letter commenting upon the observations contained therein appeared in the columns of the journal in question:

"MORMONISM AND POLYGAMY."

"TO THE EDITOR OF THE '——STAR.'

"SIR,—The article which appeared in your issue of Saturday last, by a correspondent writing from Salt Lake City, containing a description of that Mecca of the so-called Latter Day Saints, together with an account of some of their customs, seems to have 'fetched' a friend of mine residing in Lancashire, who is a 'convert,' and who has written me in highly indignant terms anent the article in question. My correspondent admits that the description of Salt Lake City, as given in the *Star,* is perfectly correct—in fact, wonderfully so, seeing that the writer of it sojourned there but one day. But the sentence in the article of your American correspondent which rouses his ire more than all the rest is that which states that 'there is not an honest Mormon, man or woman, who does not feel that polygamy is a disgrace and a shame.' My friend declares that he is acquainted with more than one person who being the child of a second, third, fourth, or even fifth wife, as the case may be, is rather proud of this circumstance than otherwise. As to the women being ashamed of polygamy, he says—'I can produce a letter written by a polygamous wife to her son who is on a mission to England, in which she reminds him, in earnest and beautiful language, of the duty her son owes to his religion, &c.' My correspondent goes on to say—'We publish in Salt Lake City a journal entitled "The Women's Exponent," whose object and aim is to defend the rights of the women of Utah and the woman-world. This paper is edited by a woman, and is contributed to solely by women who have entered polygamy many years ago and still remain in it, and the subject-matter of the articles is invariably in advocacy of plural marriages.'

'I may mention that I have myself had long conversations with my Lancashire friend with reference to the tenets of Mormonism, and with out wishing to be considered by your readers an ardent sympathiser with this singular body of people, I can assure them that there is 'more in it' than most people are aware of.—I remain,

&c., J.S."

Such advocacy—or palliation—will deceive few outside of "Zion." Polygamy should be stamped out as the plague. Successive eminent writers—male and female—in their desire to avoid being narrow-minded, have dealt far too gently with Mormonism.

DAY TWENTY-EIGHT.

At daybreak we were at the head of the Humboldt Valley, the course of which, and the river of the same name, we followed all day. Ushered in by a heavy snow-storm at an altitude of five thousand feet, the day improved to a bright but cold one. The partly cloud-hidden Humboldt Mountains on either side at one time closed in upon our track, and at others receded ten to twenty miles. Again the two walls would threaten to come together ere we should gain an outlet, the river foaming at our feet, tossed from side to side of the gorge by immense boulders intercepting its course, and wasting its fury in vain attempts to break away its prison walls.

Appearances at some points of this mountain range indicate that at one time it has had spurs extending across the valley, forming vast lakes of the waters of the river, until some mighty convulsion of nature rent the solid barriers asunder and formed passages for the roaring cascades which wash the bases of the cliffs—here five hundred to a thousand feet high. Some of the rifts are plainly water-worn, and not caused by volcanic action; for fine layers of sand appear between beds of gravel showing where the water settled and the sediment rested.

There are, however, also ample proofs of volcanic activity in byegone ages. At Wells station we got out and examined one of the springs or wells (of which there are about twenty). Water was raised from the one which we inspected for the tanks to feed the locomotives. These curious holes would not be seen excepting for the circles of rank grass around them. They are from five to six feet across, and nearly round, looking more like artificial wells than natural springs, and we looked for the heaps of soil that might have been thrown up when the well was "built" (as the Americans say). But no human digger had sunk that well. The water, slightly brackish, slowly coming to the surface, sipes off through the loose sandy soil of the valley.

Soundings had been taken to a great depth, and the report was that no bottom had been found. We took this information as being like the water—slightly brackish (***cum grano sails***), but doubted not that we looked upon the crater of a volcano long since extinct, which had thrown up the lava largely composing the surrounding face of the country, which lay about in rough blocks and in a pulverised state.

Huge pieces of granite and sandstone, shattered and thrown about in wild confusion, were also some of the reminders of the time when desolation and chaos reigned supreme; calling forth the reflection that there are other ways of employing the mind than in mines, mills, merchandise, and money. Verily, there *is* a God mightier than Mammon, among whose works the seeker after knowledge may well employ a portion of that precious talent, time, which is allotted to him!

After passing Be-o-wa-we station (literally—the gate) we observed, about eight miles to the south, jets and columns of steam rising in a line from a barren hill-side. From this line boiling muddy sulphuric water descended, desolating everything in its course, and escaping through the bogs of the plains.

Before night we skirted Humboldt Lake, into which the river empties itself. The newspapers had just recorded that the lake was fuller than had ever been known. This sheet of water, and Carson Sink (which is joined to it, excepting in summer) have, like the neighbouring smaller lakes, puzzled generations of enquirers. They have no visible outlets, and yet large rivers are discharged into them. Theories as to under ground channels are becoming discredited, actual experiment having demonstrated that the evaporation in summer is equal to six inches per day. The sun is so powerful on these lava plains in the hot season that the water evaporates quickly after it escapes from the cooling shadows of the hills. In the humid atmosphere of the greater part of the year the evaporation is reduced to a minimum, and there fore the water then covers a larger area.

A dreary desert is this expanse of hundreds of miles of lava and clay, each of which substances is as destitute of support for vegetable life as the other. No green thing meets the eye as it roams over the thousands of acres covered with dirty-white alkali. The sun's rays fall glaringly upon the barren scene; burning and withering and crushing out any attempt of Nature to introduce life. It has been contended that irrigation would render the country productive, but credible informants asserted that the experiment had been well tried with no encouraging results.

Onward we sped, reclining on our soft cushions, rolling across the alkali, and lava beds, giving but a passing thought to those who in days gone by had suffered fearfully while crossing these Nevada plains, and per chance remained as heaps of drying bones to bleach upon the and sands.

As is often the case where the surface is unproductive, great mineral wealth rewards the explorer; and valuable deposits of ore yielding lead, silver, and gold, are giving rise to thriving communities to the north and south of the main line of railroad, which are reached by new branch lines that are ever extending. A singular perversity has prompted the *hombres* (pronounced "umbreys"—a Spanish word used in these parts for "men") who had to find names for each new town or "station;" Rose Creek, and Raspberry evidently being so christened because of the impossibility of either a rose or a creek or a raspberry being found within many miles. "You Bet" speaks for itself, and "Carlin" may have some connexion with Carling Sunday (a name applied in some parts of England to the Sunday next but one before Easter) or may have been so named by some adventurous miner from the Yorkshire village of Carlin How. "Steamboat" and "Tombstone" are about as unlikely names for embryo cities as could be conceived by the most imaginative of mortals.

As we neared the Occident we found Spanish words creeping more and more into daily use, and it was gratifying to find our home terms such as "railway" and "station" occuring both in print and conversation.

The Indian loungers became more numerous, and it must have been about the time of the annual Government doling-out of new blankets and hats, for the men were sporting white felt hats with feathers stuck in them, and both sexes were comfortably enwrapped in spick-and-span blankets of gay and gaudy colours. There is a station called Winnemucca, after the Chief of the Piute Indians. The remnant of this tribe appeared to be a useless, harmless set, and were exceedingly repulsive in their looks and comportment.

All the aborigines are wards of the Government, and their affairs are administered by state-paid "agents," to whom districts are assigned. Besides the Indians scattered about among the white population, there are numbers who are consigned to "reservations," where no one is supposed to be allowed to molest them; and whence they make raids in the fine weather and return in mock penitence to be taken care of in the winter. The money employed to pension the "wards" is, by a specious fiction, supposed to be the interest upon a capitalized sum set apart as due to the aboriginal proprietors of the soil when the white men "bought" it of them!

DAY TWENTY-NINE.

Having left Reno in the early evening, our train had proceeded along the bank of the Truckee River, and, ascending a thousand and sixty feet in twenty-six miles, passed out of Nevada into California, before reaching a station called Boca. Still ascending through wild, rocky ravines, the air getting colder and colder as we got higher and higher, we came to Truckee, mounting three hundred feet in nine miles.

Here the railway officials were talking of looking out for the comet, the newspapers having set down this as the first night it might be seen with the naked eye. This same comet we never did see, although often scanning the cloudless empyrean during the time it ought to have been visible, so the astronomers had for once been wrong in their conjectures as to its probable size—a very striking tail having been predicted.

The scenery of the Sierra Nevada mountains having to be passed in the night, I am not able to describe all of it, as only sights that came under actual observation are included in my memoranda. It had been suggested that we should stay all night at Reno, and take a daylight train on to San Francisco, but the night being clear and the moon just past full, we determined to go on, retiring early, so as to be astir at three o'clock in the morning for the passage round "Cape Horn," as a bold promontory of perpendicular rock, down the very face of which the railway is "engineered," is called.

I awoke shortly after three o'clock in a snow-shed, and a precious long one it was—twenty-eight miles. There were silver moonbeams glinting through the crevices between the planks, but that was all to be seen. It was tantalizing to be thus boxed up when passing such glorious scenery. With a shriek the engine emerged from the lengthy cage, and the vision presented amply repaid the waiting for. We were tearing along high up on one side of a deep valley. No more snow; but the hills crowned with tall pines, and far, far down at the foot of the precipice spread luxuriant verdure, through which meandered a sparkling moonlit silvery stream. It was almost as light as day, a cloud less sky and transparent atmosphere enhancing the glorious light of the moon and stars.

A short stoppage was made at Summit, where we were seven thousand feet above the level of the sea; and two hundred and forty miles from San Francisco. Daylight already brightened the north-eastern horizon, against which the dark pine trees stood out clear and sharp, as we wended round the brow of the mountain where the track is cut in a sharp descent out of the very front of the precipice. An enchanting occupation it was to gaze perpendicularly down upon the tree tops and streak of river below, and we had cause for congratulation, as things had turned out, that our flit through this ravishing region was by night instead of by day.

After another hour's repose what a transformation had occurred! From the desert of Nevada we had passed the Rubicon and descended into the fruitful plains of California. At the frequent stations Indians offered for sale delicious breakfasts of strawberries grown upon the sunny slopes of the adjacent "foothills," as the undulating formation between the rugged mountains and the level country is designated; the young vines were showing their tender green shoots on tracts of vineyard spread away for miles; seas of wheat just bursting into ear refreshed our desert-strained eyes with lovely emerald; and orchards of peach and all manner of fruit-trees testified to the productiveness of this golden climate and soil. The temperature in most parts of the State is not very cold in winter nor unbearably hot in summer, and only in rare cases does the climate justify the derivation of its name—the Spanish words *caliente fornalla,* hot furnace. The very fact that many persons wear overcoats at night and sleep in blankets the year round, and that all field work from January to December is performed by labourers in their shirt sleeves, presents a better and more unequivocal illustration of the equability of the weather, perhaps, than any other incident that might be presented. There is no long cold season of frost and snow; every day's work is productive of, if not revenue, something that cannot be neutralized by the elements; the farmer has no barns or other outbuildings for stock to erect (this item alone more than counterbalancing the extra expense of fares to California for a family of from three to five); he has to lay up no piles of hay or grain for his stock, as they roam among the nutritious grasses and self-cured hay the year round. California is larger than Great Britain, being eighteen hundred miles long, and an average of two hundred broad.

We crossed the Straits of Carquinez (pronounced Kar-kee-nay) in the **Solano,** the mammoth steam ferry-boat, which has the greatest breadth of beam of any vessel afloat. She is four hundred and twenty-four feet long, one hundred and sixteen feet extreme breadth, and eighteen feet depth. She is propelled by paddle engines of two thousand effective horse power, having eight steel boilers. She is a double-ender, and at each end has four rudders constructed with coupling-rods, and every rudder has one king-pin in the centre to hold it in its place. There are four lines of rail on the boat, which will accommodate a locomotive and forty-eight goods trucks, or twenty-four of the long passenger cars.

Thirty miles of splendid views, skirting the bay, brought us to Oakland, where a pier two and a half miles long, with a double line of rails its whole length, took our train alongside of the final ferryboat for the Golden City. Our cars of passengers and baggage were quickly emptied into this magnificent steamboat, and in a few minutes we were at the landing stage upon the peninsula, on which is built the extreme western city of the American Continent—San Francisco.

Here we found omnibuses from all the prominent hotels, and tram-cars that passed by them all. Our hotel was the Palace, the largest caravansary that has yet been conceived, a town in itself, and an object of inspection for every visitor to the west, whether staying in "the house" or not. It covers three acres of ground, and the lowest down of its seven stories is twenty-seven feet high, while the rooms on the top storey are sixteen feet in height. Five elegant elevators, constantly ascending and descending, convey the twelve hundred guests to and from their apartments.

We were not long in repairing to the harbour, for the good steam yacht **Ceylon,** which was making the voyage round the world, was to sail the next morning, and we wished to have a look at her. This excursion gave us a desired knowledge of the plan of the port, and a good view of the city from the deck of the vessel, which lay at some distance from the shore. Having inspected the cabins and appointments of the ship, viewed the devices for the comfort of Mr. Fripp, of the **Graphic,** and his **co-voyageurs,** and noted their ample replenishment of the commissariat department, in the shape of flesh, fowl, fruits and fluids of the country, we bade the homeward-bound expedition God-speed, and proceeded on our tour round the bay.

Upon the bosom of the land-locked sheet of water lay such a number of goodly full-rigged sailing ships as is now rarely seen together, the steamers being confined to a few traders along the coast, and an occasional "liner" to the Asiatic continent and islands. The ***Hylton Castle*** at her moorings, flying the British ensign, was a reminder of home.

A fine graving-dock is worth mentioning, as being cut out of the solid rock, of which it is said there is not another example in the world.

Northward of the city, the peninsula upon the inner, or eastern side of which it stands, ceases in a point which forms the southern pillar of the Golden Gate—the entrance from the Pacific Ocean to the Port and the spacious bay and rivers which are navigable as far as Sacramento, Stockton, and other distant inland commercial centres.

The evening was spent in a visit to "China town" the world-renowned Chinese quarter of San Francisco. It is the dirtiest and most densely populated mass of buildings under the sun. Once the old Spanish quarter, the residence of the aristocracy of Yerba Buena (as the city was called until 1847), it has now become the location of twenty thousand Celestials who are hated by their white competitors in the labour market in a manner that had just culminated in such pressure being brought to bear upon the Congress at Washing ton that the enlightened legislature of the freest country in the world had passed an Act prohibiting further immigration from the Flowery Land for ten years. The original bill aimed at twenty years, but President Arthur had exercised his right of "veto" upon it. This, however, raised such a storm of execration from the Republicans of the western State (who swore that if the Chinamen were allowed to continue to come in they would "go Democrat" at the forthcoming presidential election) that upon the bill being a second time hurried through Congress the President had allowed it to pass, venturing, however, to alter the limit from twenty to ten years. Thus the American statesman is the slave of the lowest of the population, and a comparatively few anti-cheap-labour agitators are able to force upon the nation a law foreign to the very foundations of universal liberty upon which its constitution is framed. The news had this very day been received, so that Chinatown was in a state of bewilderment. There was not, however, such a state of utter woe as might have been expected, for the cry of "the Chinese must go" had previously reached such a pitch that frightful calamities had been hourly expected by poor John Chinaman; and now it appeared somewhat of a relief to him to know the worst and that he was to have time to gather together the forty to sixty pounds which is sufficient to take him back home and make him happy for the remainder of his natural life.

I had the benefit of the company of a friend in threading the filthy alleys of this interesting district; and it was owing to a useful custom that I had come into contact with this friend so early. Having an idea that he was in San Francisco, but having no clue but his name (which however was rather a distinctive one) I had been by no means certain of finding him out. Judge of my surprise therefore when his card was handed in shortly after our arrival at the Palace. He had seen our name in the news papers among the passengers "to arrive." At Omaha we had been visited in the train by an official who took down our "particulars" in a polite but authoritative manner which imbued us with the idea that we were bound to divulge our full history and future plans. He was simply a newsagent however for collecting in formation to telegraph to San Francisco, for two days later upon procuring newspapers from the express coming in the opposite direction we learnt that Mr. and Mrs. So-and-so, of So-and-so, England, might be expected to arrive by Friday's express!

We found such announcements usual in all the cities upon the "long routes," the "personal" columns indeed forming the most noteworthy part of the numerous editions of the daily—one-might almost call it hourly—press.

We left Chinatown after seeing the commencement of the performances at the theatres, gambling hells, and opium dens—only the commencement, for the "pieces" at the theatres last all night, and the other entertainments continue for days and nights just according to fancy.

DAY THIRTY.

Our usual early start was particularly useful here, as the morning on this part of the Pacific coast is emphatically the best part of the day, the heat inland draw-ing in through the Golden Gate towards afternoon a stiff breeze from the ocean which causes a daily mist, and considerably agitates the sandy particles of which the surface of the peninsula is composed. In the evening all is again still, bright, and, warm. Something, however must be done in the gusty, dusty part of the day, and it so befel that our first sight of the Pacific Ocean was upon this (we were told) unusually windy occasion.

Our journey to the Cliff House, a restaurant. Set on the edge of some cliffs facing the west. Was over six miles of barren country, along what was dignified with the name of a ***boulevard.*** Beneath the wide piazza of the hotel the breakers of the Pacific roared in a manner hardly compatible with the cognomen of the ocean which gave them birth, and southward along a sandy beach and northward along the rocky shore, the waves beat ceaselessly as is "their nature to" on all exposed lines of coast.

Far away on the horizon the peaks of the Farallone Islands were visible, and close at our feet, separated from the shore by a chasm of seething surf, lay the Seal Rocks, the greatest charm of the neighbourhood. The great slug-like seals, many of them as heavy as the largest ox, basked or wriggled in the sun, or gambolled in the sea around, in a manner which gave great joy to the Californians, who preserve them as jealously as do the Venetians their pigeons and the people of Constantinople their dogs. Seeing that their number is computed by thousands and that their favourite diet is salmon the outcry of the fishermen at this preservation of vermin can easily be imagined. The harsh bark of the amphibious beasts commingled strangely with the coming-and-going noise of the waters and riveted our ears as well as eyes to this singular and unexpected spot.

Returning leisurely to town we passed several cemeteries, well-kept, and with costly monuments, and rare shrubs and flowers. A noticeable feature was the ownership of beautiful burying grounds by different Societies; the Freemasons, and Oddfellows, for instance, having each resting-places of their own, where the brethren of life lie side by side in death awaiting the Day when neither oceans nor continents nor the grave itself shall divide the great Human Family. The Lone Mountain Cemetery is surmounted by a plain stone cross which is a noted landmark, being a prominent object from far out at sea.

The houses, from the humblest cabin to the stateliest mansion, are of wood, and are of the most ornamental description, only a minute inspection disclosing that the handsome cornerings, facings, and carvings above and abound the windows and doors are not, with the whole structure, of finely wrought stone. The interior of a bijou residence, surrounded by a gem of a garden, gave us an idea of the comforts of domestic life at San Francisco. The house was Inhabited by an English lady and gentleman, and their young family. The walls were papered, and there was every evidence of a homely English existence.

The calling of house-remover is a very general one in San Francisco, and parties falling in with a more desirable plot of ground for sale or hire can have their domicile transplanted *en bloc.* This operation is generally performed in the night time, to avoid interfering with the traffic. The "removers" are the only people allowed to cut the telegraph wires and otherwise disturb the public arrangements, which, of course, they have promptly to restore to proper connexion. The transfer is effected with very slight damage to fixings, a little paint and deft carpentery quickly restoring the main block and outbuildings to original symmetry.

Those inevitable eyesores, the telegraph posts, are in the western metropolis as little objectionable as possible, by being made of dressed timber and neatly and quietly painted. The telephone is thoroughly utilised: from the Cliff House we had a long conversation with our friends in the city for a nominal charge. At a lawyer's office, beneath the ordinary paraphernalia of the instrument, was a dial marked "messenger, fire, hack, police, doctor," &c. All required was to put the pointer to the desired word, and in an incredibly short space of time the doctor would arrive up the elevator, or the carriage or fire-engine would be at the street door, as the case might be.

A change in the common computation of money had become observable as the west was approached, founded upon an extinct coin of twelve and a half cents (an eighth of a dollar) called a "bit." Small fares and commodities up to a dollar in value were spoken of as worth a "bit," "six bits," and so on. As the actual change could not in many cases be given, there was supposed to be a give-and-take (the Californian having the "take," you bet, when a stranger, was in the case), *e.g.,* if you had only a dime (ten cents) you were allowed to pay it for a "bit;" but if you put down a quarter (twenty-five cents) in payment for a bit's worth you only took up ten cents change. Hence the expressions "large bit" and "small bit," meaning in practice fifteen cents and ten cents respectively. They know nothing of this free and easy computation in the Eastern States. The royal indifference of the Westerns to the circulating medium is something superb. It might naturally be asked, why not use the one and two cent coins? Answer: Because there are none here. In a street-car I dropped a solitary copper coin that had bothered my pocket for some days, and there I let it lie—glad to be rid of the useless disc. A gentleman asked if he might have it, as he had not seen one for years. He said they were sorry that ever they had allowed the monetary unit to get below ten cents (fivepence), as fractions were so bothering!

All Spanish names and expressions are proudly retained, and you must never be heard using the irreverent abbreviation 'Frisco, the only curtailment admissible to the dignity of the citizens being that which they frequently use, "San Fran."

One of the most remarkable buildings in the city is the Safe Deposit Block. This magnificent edifice is of ornamental stone and iron, five stories in height. The walls are connected by immense wrought iron girders, from basement to roof. Each stone in the construction is secured by two anchors to the heavy interior brick walls. In-side, are erected immense steel vaults containing four thousand six hundred small safes built in solid tiers within the impregnable masonry. Surrounding this mammoth vault is a corridor, completely enclosed by a net-work of iron and steel, and there continually, night and day, the armed patrol, under the charge of the Super-intendent, make their rounds. On entering the vault-room an imposing sight greets the eye. The vaults stand out as a monument of mechanical skill, impressing one with this gigantic undertaking, called forth by the constant advancement of this wonderful city. The different avenues, the massive doors, the sumptuous offices for renters, and parlours for ladies, give an idea of great strength and grandeur. The renter exclusively holds the only key that will open his safe, which key will fit no other safe, as no two locks are alike. The renter, before being admitted to the vault, must be identified by the proper officer. He unlocks and locks his own safe, but only after one of the patrol (without whom none can enter) has unlocked the escutcheon which covers the lock. The lock is changed with every change of renter. The company has five inside patrols, who are citizens of known reputation, long residence and undoubted integrity. They are uniformed and armed. Every half hour, day and night, a communication is passed between the armed watch of the building and the patrol within. A telegraphic report is also sent half hourly from within to the police head quarters.

It may be asked to whom the safe depository may be useful? A pamphlet given to us sum marised them thus:—All small or large holders of Government coupon bonds; retired capita lists, desks being provided where cash-boxes may be opened;

manufacturers, mechanics, tradesmen, clergymen, physicians, and other business and professional men; families, widows and single women; for family plate, jewellery, family relics or souvenirs, securities or papers of value; the large class of thrifty persons whose surroundings are unfavourable to the safe-keeping of valuables; lawyers and their clients, whose papers in a suit, if lost by fire, might not be replaceable; masters of vessels, or others from home; colleges, academies, lodges, and other institutions, literary, benevolent, social or religious, with securities or papers of value; persons having no bank account, for bank drafts or specie temporarily; foreigners, transient in the city, with money, jewellery, securities or valuable papers; Americans residing abroad, who may leave their securities here, the interest to be collected and remitted; holders of valuable papers, or articles for minor children; churches, for communion plate; duplicate marriage records, etc.; assignment; evidences of marriage, birth or death; valuable letters, manuscripts, or papers to be opened after the death of the writer; collections of coins, copper plates, costly lades, etc., etc.

The tramway system is most perfect. On California-street there are four lines of rails, and departures every minute from all points. At one time I counted from the portal of the Palace Hotel thirty-eight cars—an imposing array. In the hilly parts "dummy" cars are employed which are drawn along by an endless rope enclosed in a casing level with the road way, a slit in which admits a lever worked by the conductor of the "dummy," by which the starting and stopping is accomplished with great ease. The motive power is a stationary engine of five hundred horse power.

During our brief sojourn three items of news arrived which were of great moment to various sections of the inhabitants, The regrettable fate of Lieutenant De Long and the "Jeannette" expedition caused all flags to be hoisted half-mast. Mrs De Long resided in San Francisco, and the ill-fated vessel had started from thence. Joy reigned (excepting in Chinatown) at the President having signed the bill staying Chinese immigration; and an unmistakeable feeling of satisfaction (spreading beyond the Irish themselves) was evinced at the dastardly murders in Phœnix Park, Dublin. It was, palpably necessary for the Land League cause that the show of disclaiming countenance of the outrage should be paraded from the "centres" in the States, but hourly contact with the people proved its hollowness. Some—to say the least—very remarkable "coincidences" occurred. There was nothing very surprising about the rapidity with which the news reached the Pacific coast, for every item connected with Ireland had been known by us daily, the same as if at home, and the newspapers gave verbatim reports of every day's debates at Westminster; then again the European night left the cables at liberty for this horrible Saturday evening's news to be whisked under sea and over land from Ireland to sympathetic America. But it *was* strange that a monstre Land League meeting should be taking place, which did not close, until the chairman was able to read the (of course unexpected) telegram, which, after being duly cheered by the audience, was in proper course deprecated by the chairman, and the crime described as the work of "some crazy loon, who, he was sure, would have no connexion with any organized body of Irishmen." This statement can be verified by reference to the San Franciscan newspapers of the following morning, Sunday the seventh of May, 1882. As I proceeded along Montgomery Street towards the hotel about eleven o'clock at night (seven o'clock Sunday morning, English time) my friend and I were struck with groups of excited people crowded round the newspaper offices reading by the electric light the following announcement chalked upon huge black boards—"Lord Frederick Cavendish and Mr Bourke, Under Secretary, were assassinated this evening in Phœnix Park, Dublin." After the first cold shiver and feeling of utter helplessness, the impulse was to cast around for sympathy. When I found words I exclaimed, "It cannot be; it cannot be!" A big man with Hibernian accent (they keep the brogue out there for generations) turned upon me, and remarked, emphatically, "Why the—shouldn't it be?" The crowd commencing to focus our knot, my friend whispered, "Let us make tracks," which we were fortunately able to do, amid the mutterings of the crowd. Reflection showed us that had an unwise altercation been entered into, the consequences might have been serious. I don't suppose that greater danger would have existed in the midst of the wildest savages than in the heart of that civilized community, among fellow-creatures of one's own blood and tongue. Hoping to find some Englishman with whom to get the relief of a little conversation before retiring to bed, I repaired to the bar of the Palace. There evidently was not a Britisher there, for my remark that "This is awful news from Ireland" only brought forth the tardy response from a gentlemanly looking American, "Wal, you Britishers have used Ireland tarnation badly." So to bed, and to disturb the slumbers of my better-half by a recital of Britain's troubles and my own. The conductor of the elevator did say it was "too bad," but assured me that a war with England "would make every working man in the United States a soldier," and added as a parting shot as I meekly bade him good night: "We would have had a go at you over that Fisheries Question if we'd had a navy!"

DAY THIRTY-ONE.

While we were at Boston considerable unction had been laid to the New England conscience by the fact that the puritan city had scored a Sunday's attendance at places of worship of three out of every four inhabitants. So it had been ascertained by the more or less reliable expedient of the now fashionable "religious census." I am afraid that if a like test had been applied to the flourishing Pacific port the result would have been of a very different character. We had to take a Sabbath day's journey to Stockton in order to make that place the point of departure for an early start on Monday morning for the Yosemite Valley, and the bands of music and parties of picnic folk which crowded steamboat and rail showed anything but a strict Sabbatarianism.

A visit to the handsome offices of the Southern Pacific Railway Company had made all right as to tickets and baggage. By the admirable American system, by which you can take your tickets at any time and for any time and "check" your baggage to various stations on the route as you may require the pieces, the journey across the continent to Quebec was arranged as easily as taking a ticket for a round tour to the Scottish Lakes. The published time-tables state the fares, so that you are all ready with the needful when you go to the counter. "Two for Quebec." Accustomed as the hard-faced official doubtless was to big things, this brief request momentarily threw him off his guard, and he remarked "That's a tall order, mister." (The fare was about sixty pounds.) Observing, however, that I had the roll of greenbacks ready, he lapsed into imperturbability and handed me the three and a half feet of ticket, to be used up in pieces as we went along. Although our journey, taking a southern route, was fully twenty-four hours longer than by the most direct line, the fare was the same, the competing railroads generally adjusting matters in this fashion to neutralise the competition. In most instances a ticket will allow you to break your journey when and where you like, and will remain good for any length of time. In this particular case the fare was understood to be especially low for certain "special limited" tickets. Thus I found that to carry out my programme I should over step by two days the limit of the ticket and become liable for sixteen dollars more.

The courteous passenger manager, Mr. Goodall, to whom I had explained the case at the hotel the night before, had promised to send on to Madera Station a note making our tickets unlimited ones, a kindness which in due course was fulfilled. Next to arrange a sleeping-car; for, although we were not going to join the main line until the following Friday evening it was necessary to secure berths, and comfortable ones, at the starting station. Shown the printed plan of the Palace car for the date in question, I selected double lower ones, which, sure enough, after hundreds of miles of rough mountain travelling, we were fortunate enough to occupy.

Arrived at Stockton, we found a staid, solid town, with thirteen churches, some banks, and fair public buildings. Upon one substantial edifice was inscribed, "First National Bank of Stockton." The place was not named, as is sometimes stated (so said the directory), after a "small" town of that name in the North of England, but after General Stockton, who assisted in the capture of California. The country around is very flat, and is immensely productive of wheat. The soil is adobe, a shining black loam, which makes an almost imperishable sun-baked brick, of which most of the houses are built, and then plastered. What are sometimes no ornament to the Californian landscape are here made as picturesque as possible, namely, the windmills working the artesian wells. Every house has one, and the numerous wands are prettily coloured, and, although looking rather gimcrack, they are far from ugly appendages to the widely spread-out buildings and gardens. The guide books dignify Stockton with the title of the City of Windmills, and Don Quixote would indeed have found here a rare field for glory.

Attendance at a pretty little Episcopal church wound up the day, and we heard an excellent discourse on Consistency, which rather struck home, as we remembered how in the early part of the day we had exemplified to our own convenience that "the Sabbath was made for man."

DAY THIRTY-TWO.

The train from Stockton to Milton went over a line that was the "tapering off" of the rail road system, our car being one of a train composed mainly of goods and cattle waggons. The engine was fired with wood, and the arrangements altogether were such as to throw some doubt upon our punctual arrival at the station for the "stage"—a generic term for all vehicles plying upon regular services. Nor were our fears altogether groundless, for after getting over about half of the thirty miles, slower and slower became our speed, until a dead stop ensued. Nothing but waving grass and wheat was to be seen to the horizon, excepting, towards the east, the distant mountains. No fence bounded the track, and the tall grasses were blown by a strong breeze directly across the plates, so that the driving-wheels of the locomotive would not grip the rail. All hands turned out to pull up the grass ahead of the train, and then a few yards would be gained, but whenever a slight upward gradient was come to the operation had to be repeated. The "stage" was waiting at Milton for us and the mails; and after the driver, had "cuss'd" our train, and said that an old bullock team could make better time, he drove off towards the hills with only three passengers for the Yosemite, and another for "the mines."

While jolting over the foothills to the first stopping place, Copperopolis, ample opportunity was afforded of studying the extent and effect of irrigation. Most of the streams dry up in the summer so as to make the land of little value for grazing or cultivation, but ingenious expedients are used to make the most of Nature's stores of the precious fluid. Where the well supply is unavailable a supply is often brought from a great distance by "V flumes." These flumes are formed of two planks joined in the form of the letter V, supported on tressles or laid along the hills to the correct level. We saw one fifty-three miles long, which floated down lumber from the mountains. Great care has to be taken in constructing the bends, so as not to cause a jam among the pieces of wood that are swimming down, men being in constant attendance to keep the course clear. Water for washing for gold is often conveyed by dexterous feats of engineering into curious corners by means of flumes, and we came across them in all positions with their trickling threads of water, by the aid of which solitary miners were extracting the coveted yellow specs from the gravelly soil. Blackberries are cultivated on the lower slopes of the mountains and yield good returns. A gentleman who had been a hopeless invalid in England was able here to plough and harrow all day, sustained by the salubrious climate, and employed his evenings in directing the water from the flume through little ditches so that the carefully watered roots should cause a plentiful crop of brambles.

We changed horses at Copperopolis, which settlement was only a shade of its former greatness, the mining industry which gave it its name having retired further into the mountains. The road now became wild in the extreme, many miles being passed without the sign of the hand or foot of man or of tame beast ever having been there, excepting the wheel-marks of our rugged track, or "trail," as the apologies for roads now commenced to be termed. Our bones not yet having become accustomed to be rattled about, this first day's jolting caused considerable inconvenience, and many a fine view lost half its effect by our having to hold on with both hands to avoid being pitched overboard. The vehicles must be of marvellous construction to stand the heavy strain, for if a wheel or brake or axle were to give way then nothing could save the expedition from utter annihilation. The springs are a wonderful contrivance and admirably adapted for their purpose. They are simply immense leathern straps upon which the body of the stage is suspended— huge strips of well-tanned hide of many thicknesses, allowing the vehicle to hang at something like a level, irrespective of the positions of the wheels. The six horses are of the mustang type and seem calculated to go at full gallop either up or down a house-top as might be required of them. But the drivers; what shall be said of the drivers? At first it seems as if their performance were sheer madness. You say to yourself that there cannot be any method or discretion in such dare-devil driving; that the fellow must be drunk or desperate and has made up his mind to let matters take their chance. But you soon learn to appreciate the iron nerve, the rivetted attention, and the consummate judgment, that enable him to have such powerful command over those game little horses; and in awe you sit beside him, only venturing to break the silence by offering him a cigar when the horses are being watered at one of the many mountain rills that cross the trail. Sweet were those drinks of icy water to ourselves also, and the five minutes stretching of the legs and ability to hold a connected conversation was very acceptable. Five consecutive days of this staging convinced us that these Californian Jehus must be the very finest drivers in the world. They have their own lives as well as yours in their hands, besides the responsibility of the mails, and often valuable treasure, and no set of men are more worthy of the trust reposed in them. They are nearly all young men—little more than boys some of them—and they never drink on their journeys (if indeed they take any alcohol at all, which I doubt). They are well paid, don't bother you with much "sir" or "madam," and neither expect nor receive any tips.

Between two high ridges a delicious sight gladdened our eyes. A comfortable homestead was nestled in a garden of deep green trees. This sheltered spot enjoyed a liberal supply of water and an immunity from winter's snows. The sturdy settler who greeted us and watered our horses had turned its advantages to best account. He had fig-trees, peaches, and orange-trees. Upon the latter last year's fruit still hung ripening, while the new blossom was almost ready to burst forth.

Another interval of heavy ascents and descents and we came to Chinese Camp, a village, only part of the population of which were natives of China, whatever may have once been the case. The banks of the river Stanislaus showed signs of old gold-washing "claims," and some of more recent use. At a point on the river Tuolumne a single house only marked the spot where Nelsonville had been washed away by a flood.

Here was a man at the river's edge washing for gold, and I gave him a "bit" for five minutes' results, but not a spec of the precious metal appeared. Our driver's opinion was that the two fishing-rods which the miner had stuck in the river bank to provide him with his evening meal would yield him a better return than his quest for the dross.

These rivers are simply torrents following the gorges between the mountains, and our "stage" skirted or traversed their beds for a while, and anon wended over precipitous passes, only to be found once more fording or bridging the stream.

Threading the course of one defile, it looked ahead as if there could be no exit, the river broadening and filling with its here deep and rapid waters the whole breadth of the cleft between the rocks. We suddenly came upon a rude habitation, and a sort of raft moored close beside it. This proved to be a ferryboat, upon which we were to cross, and well it served its purpose. A stout wire rope was stretched from side to side of the stream, about six feet above the surface of the water, along which ran two large pulleys, to which each end of the raft was attached by short ropes. As soon as the old man in attendance had got stage and horses "all aboard," he tightened the rope at the end of the craft farthest from the shore, so that the current rushing past the oblique surface presented to it caused us to glide rapidly to the other side, the blocks running gaily along the guiding rope. When we had ascended a ledge that disclosed itself for our passage up the cliff, we observed the strange vessel—the lengths of the pulley-ropes having been reversed—quickly convey the ancient mariner back to his peaceful and lonely abode.

Before dark we ascended the dry bed of a river, literally without any "trail" at all, the stage simply bumping away over the boulders where the driver could pick out the smallest ones. This was the very ***beau ideal*** of a place for "washing" in a gold-seeking country, and soon we came upon scattered diggers, most of them Chinamen, engaged in "placer mining" as it is called here. Most of the operations were carried on over ground that had long since been riddled by early miners, but very little satisfies the Celestials, and here again we were informed that as small a sum as two hundred dollars of savings enables them to go back to China and live independently ever after. Another method of gold-mining is by the sinking of shafts; and at some points we could see or hear boring, blasting, digging, and "pickaxing" going forward, large heaps of débris showing how the ground beneath had been honeycombed.

Tired and shaken, we arrived at a station called "Priest's," where a homely Scottish lady took us in hand, and we were told that we would be called at four o'clock in the morning to breakfast, and resume our journey.

DAY THIRTY-THREE.

We had a grand Californian breakfast and were on our way with six fine horses before five o'clock. Similar driving to that of the previous day brought us by ten o'clock to a settlement where we were invited to pay a dollar each for "dinner." Although ready for a slight refection by way of luncheon, we resented the idea of dining at this unfashionable hour, but on learning that this was the last habitation we should pass before late in the evening, we were fain to do our best to lay in a "square meal." There were provisions and water in our waggon in case of an enforced camp for the night, but they were not to be touched yet awhile.

Our ups and downs resulted by midday in our attaining an elevation of six thousand three hundred feet above the sea-level, and our track was now rarely clear of snow. The summit was a clearance called Crane Flat, and the summer occupant of the "desirable residence" eligibly situated thereon had just that very morning succeeded in digging himself into his snow-preserved mansion for the coming "season." He provided us with a drop of decent whiskey, and we plunged into an afternoon's work of pushing through the softening snow. A team that had come through in the morning when the snow was frozen had got along pretty well, but a hot forenoon had made it very bad going.

It now transpired that the stage the day before had stuck fast, and the passengers had to camp until the moon had risen and the snow hardened in the middle of the night. We were many a time within an ace of a like fate, but by all turning out and walking over the worst parts, and our team plodding gamely on, we escaped with nothing worse than wet feet and a little fatigue.

The stage had been plying for four weeks, but it had been on runners—sleighing, in fact. Then had followed a week of driving the horses in snow-shoes—pieces of wood, eleven inches by eight, fastened on to the hoofs by iron clamps. The condition of the road now rendered all these expedients of no assistance; the poor brutes simply had to plunge on, often up to their bellies in the holding mass, sometimes falling, and sometimes lying down of their own accord for a rest. The conveyance frequently lay over upon its side as one wheel came on a softer spot than the opposite ones, and every few minutes had to be dug out by the labourers who were employed in endeavouring to clear the road. We passed through the Tuolumne Grove of **Wellingtonia gigantea,** but as this mammoth vegetation will be described later on upon our visit to the more numerous Mariposa Grove, I will dismiss it for the present, excepting to say that the wretched state of the road compelled us to stick to the old "trail" instead of taking a short detour now used, as it allows horses, stage, and load of passengers to pass through a tunnel cut through the trunk of one of the monstre trees.

As the sun sank in the west the snowy part of our journey was at last left behind, and, our vehicle intact and horses in wonderful trim, we commenced the descent of a steep road into a wild, undulating region. But where was the Yosemite Valley? We knew by the pictures we had seen that it was something very different to anything we saw yet. Apparently just beneath us (but in reality a considerable distance off) opened a great chasm, the bottom of it at first invisible. Yes, ***down there*** was the wondrous valley of all valleys! Not only had we to go to the verge of that gorge, but ***into*** it; and deep, deep down we could now discern that it ***had*** a bottom. The deceptive distance was quickly lessened, and our senses became aware of a novel sensation as we beheld the effect, in a vast mountain country, of a rift a mile deep, an average of only a mile wide, and scarcely seven miles in length!

Entranced by the dangerous task awaiting us of having to drive down the face of perpendicular cliffs, we passed unheeded the interesting formation of the rocks close to us—a wild boulder district, with huge stones spread about, their sizes and shapes varying from those of the dome of St. Paul's to the similarity of an elephant, resemblances that gave rise to high-sounding and extraordinary names.

Arrived at the edge of the valley or gulche, we entered upon a zigzag trail and fancied at times, as we were whirled along at an alarming pace, that we could throw a stone to the opposite wall, which was in reality a mile off! One or two horse-trails had been until recently the only passes among these precipices, but now there were three roads of bold and dexterous engineering, each admitting a single team and waggon, but with no passing places. The uninhabited vicinity and the meagre traffic render easy the working of the necessary system by which the inward commerce occupies the trails in the evening and the outward in morning. Any chance vehicles are duly heralded and are warned at the "stations" that they must draw up at a convenient "siding" until the regular services have passed. The stages, horses, roads, bridges, ferries, and stations, on each route are in the hands of a separate company, outsiders having to pay toll.

Darkness enveloped the scene as we arrived at the flat floor of the valley and sped along a sandy track beneath lofty pines to one of the three hotels, where we turned in to rest and await the bursting glories of sunrise.

DAY THIRTY FOUR.

Daylight disclosed the source of a loud continuous roar which we had heard during the night, for right in front of our window wag the Yosemite Fall. The stream takes a vertical leap of fifteen hundred feet and then an unbroken fall of six hundred feet and finally a plunge of four hundred feet to the bottom of the chasm. The plentiful supply of water at this season gave the appearance of a uninterrupted water fall of over twenty-five hundred feet. It only requires the height of St. Paul's Cathedral (three hundred and seventy feet to the top of the cross) to be kept in mind to form an approximate idea of the stupendous proportions of this extraordinary region. We were facing the north, and a little to the east rose a bold peak three thousand feet above the valley. It must be borne in mind that the bed of the valley, through which the river Merced flows, receiving the waters from all the falls, is more than four thousand feet above the level of the sea, and that all the altitudes are given, starting from that already lofty elevation.

The expeditions to the various points of vantage can only be made on horseback, the ladies being compelled to stride the saddle in the same manner as gentlemen.

There is very little débris at the base of the encircling rocks, the granite of which they are composed being scarcely wearable by water. The places at the top where the streams tumble over remain as sharp as the other edges of the cliff. The air, however, has a slight decomposing effect upon the stone, and this gives a shining surface to the perpendicular walls, and accounts for the fine sand which forms the holding for the trees and other vegetation of the bottom. This wear widens the space between the sides at the rate of a minute fraction of an inch per annum. Pines of centuries' growth and more than two hundred feet high appear against the precipitous cliffs as plants of asparagus beneath a, high garden-wall. Professor Whitney says, "Many waterfalls surpassing the most frequented in Europe are left unvisited because there are so many other wonders to occupy attention." Nearly all the falls, however, are dried up in summer, and it requires a visit in May, as ours was, to see them to full advantage, The Bridal Veil, a sheet of water thirty yards across, drops clean over a ledge nine hundred feet high, the falling liquid becoming disintegrated into fleecy ringlets of spray, which rapidly resolve themselves into a gushing torrent at the spectator's feet. A magnificent double rainbow adorns the face of this beautiful cataract every afternoon. The Virgin's Tears Creek at the opposite side of the valley makes a fine fall of three thousand three hundred feet, enclosed in a deep recess of the rock. This is a very petted fall, and is rarely to be relied upon, but the virgin must have been very naughty or else weeping for joy that day, for she shed her tears copiously enough upon us. There are half-a-dozen other large falls of similar dimensions to those described, and innumerable "ribbon falls," whose fantastic motions, as wafted by the wind over the face of the smooth granite, form an interesting feature in a Spring inspection of this enchanting gorge. The waterfalls were all more copious in the evening, for during the night the melting process on the surrounding mountains ceased, and the collecting river Merced was consequently two feet higher at night than in the morning.

Highest of the mountains is Cloud's Rest, over six thousand feet; and next, the South Dome, five thousand, the Indian name for which means Goddess of the Valley. The Indians; who were unfollowed by white men here until the year 1851, have beautiful names for every point; thus Yo-Semité means Great Grizzly Bear. The following English names of various parts of the scenery are sufficiently descriptive: Round Tower, North Dome, Glacier Point, Cap of Liberty, Three Graces, Three Brothers, Sentinel Rock, and Cathedral Spires. The last-mentioned are wonderfully like a Gothic cathedral, and not, as is often the case, suggestive of anything but the object named after. There are a centre tower, and gigantic twin spires of almost identical shape and proportion, but the king of all is the stupendous, Spanish-named, El Capitan. This majestic "pillar of the earth" stands unequalled in giant glory, and as we gazed in awe upon it the Psalmist's apostrophe of the great Architect occurred forcibly to us,—

Before the hills in order stood, Or Earth received her name, From everlasting thou art God, To endless years the same!

In an alcove a thousand feet up the face of this "Captain" is a pine of a hundred feet high, which presents, when viewed through a field-glass, the picture of a perfect tree growing upon a ledge, which must afford the merest scrap of support.

The Utes, or Digger Indians, still camp in the valley, and are not discounte-

nanced, as they are inoffensive, and are one of the amusements of visitors. They mi-
grate to regions more clear of snow for the winter, and leave their stores of acorns
until their return in spring. Their acorn "hives," holding many tons, are formed of
branches of trees, and are elevated on poles out of harm's way. When required for
use the acorns are shelled and pounded into a meal, of which cakes are made to be
eaten by the aborigines with their fish or flesh. Trout are abundant in the river, and
it is strange that no one but the Indians can here catch them in numbers. This they
do, and sell them to the hotels. We could not have any, because "the Indians had
not come in yet."

From October to March the Yosemite is closed to the outer world, excepting
such slender communication as is kept up by means of a postman who, on snow-
shoes, makes his way across the mountains with "the mails." During the past winter,
however, even this fitful service had been suspended. The practice of staying in the
valley over winter is getting more favoured, no less than thirty-five persons having remained in their houses during the snow-bound months just expired. Plenty
of provisions for man and beast had been stored, and everybody, including women
and children, had disported on snow-shoes and in sleighs, shooting and trapping
game to their hearts' content. Many valuable skins were secured, consisting of bear,
wolverine, silver fox, &c. Those hotels and houses which were entirely closed and
snow-buried had to be opened out and set in order as early as possible, and wondrous feats of walking and sleighing were reported as having been performed by
entering in March of the present year; the valley itself being clear.

During some winters there are periods of comparatively open weather: in January, 1878, A, Pendarves Vivian, Esq., M.P., F.G.S., managed to drive into the valley, but was glad to get out of it again after a night's rest, to avoid a threatened
snowstorm. He found the proprietor of Leidig's Hotel "at home," and "mine host"
exploded a dynamite cartridge in honour of the abnormal visitor.

DAY THIRTY-FIVE.

Nine passengers filled our strong light stage, and we started while it was yet
dawn, a jovial party, from the Yosemite Valley Hotel for Big Tree Station, twenty-

five miles away.

The only preparations needed were against the dust, the perennial sunshine at this season rendering precautions against rain unnecessary. Our six horses rattled us merrily along the valley to the steep winding trail forming the exit, and, after a tortuous ascent, pauses were made at Artist's Point and Inspiration Point to drink in once more the delicious views of the arcadia we were leaving, now bathed in the sheen of the glittering morning sun. The morning and evening effects in California are very grand, the orb of day rising and setting clean against the horizon of sea or land without any traces of haze or cloud.

In hours of trouble, and when under the influence of "the blues," one is apt to exclaim, "What have I done that can deserve such utter misery as this?" And here the compensating balance of a kind Providence gave us an experience in the opposite direction; the delightful sensations attending these early morning starts in the life-giving atmosphere being like a foretaste of heaven or an earnest of the delights of paradise; prompting the reflection, "What have we poor mortals done to merit such happiness?"

We passed Fort Neptune, a hut inhabited by a sportsman known as Father Neptune, and saw that worthy working in his garden with his rifle slung at his back. He informed us that recently he had killed two bears, and we were able to tell him that there was more like game in store, as, only the night previous, five hogs had been killed by a "grizzly" in the enclosure belonging to the one butcher of the Yosemite. The denizens of the valley expressed confidence in bagging him, as his nightly depredations betokened a growing temerity that would prove fatal to him. Rattlesnakes were plentiful, and our driver adroitly left one a writhing corpse, killed by a stroke of his whip.

The forest was carpeted with brilliant wild flowers, and the air was fragrant with ten thousand blossoms. Prominent amongst the gems which bedecked the sward was the beautiful snow-plant, whose bright crimson cone protruded with rare contrast through the thinning sheets of snow, or blossomed for a day uncovered before being burnt up by the glare of the springtide sun. The flowering shrubs were magnificent, the density of every colour being remarkable. The many-tinted manzanita and madrone mingling with bushes of wild lilac, plum and a hundred others—conspicuous amongst which was the treacherous, crimson-leaved "poison oak"—left an impression upon the mind's retina that time can never efface. Then, towering over all like giant shades and protectors, were the lofty monarchs of the forest! Stately, straight as arrows and supple as bows they heeded not the blasts of winter nor the droughts of summer, but from age to age, so long as left alone in their primeval pride, they pointed heavenwards their dark green plumes! Their varieties, embracing red, yellow, and sugar pines, and cedar, spruce, and common firs, exhibited every shade of foliage.

An alloy to our joy was the frequent sight of fine trees destroyed by fire, some laid prostrate, others still erect, with charred trunks and remnants of branches, testifying to the wantonness of campers, whose embers had fired the scrub and spread the devouring element to the inflammable resinous bark of the trees. Very heavy fines are upon the statute-book for such criminal carelessness, and there was a manifest determination among the settled inhabitants to assist the State officers in bringing the offenders-to punishment. We passed by a "claim" where a clearance was being made by the help of fire, and it occurred to us that even this-legitimate use of it ought to be very jealously guarded from abuse. Only the preceding summer the whole of the timber in the Yosemite valley had been endangered by some sheepmen having caused a conflagration along the edge of the overhanging cliffs, one burning twig or spark from which might have transferred into a hades the paradise beneath.

At Point Lookout we had a splendid panorama of the Chouchilly Mountains, and our Jehu showed us a notch in a tree, ten feet above the ground, which he had cut three weeks before, to mark the level at which he had driven a sleigh over the snow.

We partook of luncheon at Clarke's Ranche, where we ultimately stayed overnight, and took a fresh team for the Mariposa Grove of Big Trees, one of the real original Wonders of the World of our school-books. A laconic driver rather irritated a gentleman among us who volunteered to ply the reticent one with whiskey from his flask if I would undertake to "draw" him while under its influence. It was all in vain, until, adopting tactics savouring of Mark Twain, I made a remark that brought him down from his pinnacle of indifference. It was in this wise. The guides and drivers thereabouts are genuinely in love with their scenery and pet show-places, and do not perform their part in a mere prefunctory manner. This imperturbable individual had, beneath his Californian hide, the ***amour patrie*** of his kind, and drew up his team in majestic style at the foot of the Grizzly Giant (as one of the mammoth trees is called), and with a wave of his whip turned a beaming countenance upon us, as much as to say "There!" I eyed this specimen of the biggest thing in trees in the world and said, "Wal, I guess we have bigger tree than that in our backyard home!" The change in his face brought a hearty peal of laughter from all, and thenceforth Mr. driver was as communicative as his nature would allow, his opening comment being "Wal, stranger, if you got bigger tree nor yon in your country, you must come from a good way off."

The Americans hate the name of ***Wellingtonia,*** and say that these trees are properly the ***sequoia gigantea***—some having gone so far as-to name them ***Washingtonia.*** Seeing that the trees are in one of their "national parks," it is only fair to let them call them what they like.

In the twilight we visited an encampment of the Coldstring Indians, and interviewed their stoical and uninteresting chief, Chickabon, who we all agreed was a more desirable acquaintance when we were within hailing distance of our "hotel," and our party outnumbered his, than he would have been in the depth of the forest under different circumstances.

DAY THIRTY-SIX.

A drive of seventy-two miles was requisite to reach the Central Pacific Railroad at Madera, and the same company took stage at sunrise to accomplish it. Being still four thousand feet above the sea, tortuous paths and perilous descents had to be traversed before we reached the plains. Here and there swollen streams had to be forded that caused many a jolting and slight wetting.

For many miles never a habitation was come in sight of, and hours elapsed without a single human being besides ourselves being visible. Traces of the ***genus homo*** were, however, fallen in with, unmistakeable evidence of the recent presence of mankind being a parcel of trout, weighing about twenty pounds, which, tied up in a piece of cotton fabric, lay a suspicious-looking bundle by the wayside. Upon its contents being disclosed, the first impression was one of gratification at such a useful "find." But it was not ours, and the enticing "perishable goods" were placed as much sheltered from the sun as possible, in case the unconscious loser or confiding depositor should return to claim his or her own. The chances were that the rightful owner was some Indian squaw (for the redskins make their women do all the work) who had been early astir that morning engaged in piscatorial pursuit.

The road was still only a single track and as we got to more frequented country and became more liable to encounter other vehicles, an occasional pedestrian would come towards us, the ***avant courier*** of some approaching team, come to arrange a passing place. An interesting cavalcade we passed was formed of three immense freight waggons. The first one was drawn by six mules, the leaders having Russian-like appendages over their heads, from which ten jingling bells gave warning to approaching travellers. The other two waggons were drawn by ten bullocks each, the driving of which was a laborious task, and how they wound round the sharp turns of the rocks, or how any but the two "wheelers" could be of any use at critical points, were puzzles to all of us.

In crossing—many miles to the southward of our outward journey—the foothills lying between the Rocky Mountains and the level country to the westward, we again passed several vineyards. This interesting branch of agriculture we were informed was liable to be overdone. Fair port and sherry, and good claret and brandy, were made, principally by European vinters, who had been imported, but as the vinous liquids of commerce are not ruled in value by merit alone, the prices realized were barely remunerative. At the hotels the native wines always figured on the card at much lower prices than foreign brands; and as for the brandies, they had not yet had time to attain age to test their merits.

The little phylloxera, which has played such havoc with the vines of Europe from time to time, was as yet unknown in California at the time of our visit.

The last portion of the stage journey was across seventeen miles of flat land, the pasturage dried up, and the prospect of wheat harvest on this particular section almost ***nil.*** It was melancholy to see in this glorious corn-growing weather and country, mile after mile of ground upon which all the energies and patience of the tiller and sower had been expended, with scarcely a blade visible; nor would there be, for the fixed dry season had now set in and there would be no more rain until the harvest in more fortunate localities was cut and thrashed. This unusual misfortune was the result of an almost unprecedently droughty spring, succeeded by an opening dry-season marked by persistent strong winds, which licked up every vestige of moisture and were still blowing, causing us to suffer from the dust as if pursuing our way through a barren desert instead of one of the ordinarily most productive regions in the world.

The normal climate renders the State of California a farmers' paradise, the regularity of the seasons being such that his operations can be carried on with the minimum of uncertainty as to results. Favorable seed-time, followed by gentle rains, gives place to the glorious golden summer during which the grain grows, ripens, and is garnered. After it is cut the owner leaves it standing in the field and goes to Sacramento or San Francisco to sell it, returning to thrash it out and put it into the bags in which it finds its way to the miller near home, or across the sea to distant England.

A wretched cluster of shanties is Madera, but soon the welcome train drew up that was to carry us southwards to the orange groves and rose gardens of Los Angeles and to the very confines of Mexico.

DAY THIRTY-SEVEN.

During the night we had slept through the famous Loop Tunnel, where, to suit the exigencies of the construction of the line, the road is made to describe a circle and go under and over itself. This is wrongly stated in some guide-books to be the only case of the kind in the world; there being at least two others, one in the United States, and the other in descending by the Roumanian State Railway from the Carpathians towards the Austrian frontier on the Danube.

The "City of the Angels" lies at the southern base of the Sierra Santa Monica mountains and is completely embowered in foliage; being irrigated from the Los Angeles river by windmills. Vineyards, orange and lemon orchards, and lovely gardens and groves meet the eye at every turn, while magnificent plantations stretch away as far as sight can ken.

The morning meal in the cool and cleanly *buffet* had the advantage of tropical plants, fruits, and beverages, combined with the homeliness of the Anglo-Saxon language. Nothing save the inscriptions upon the signboards, and the tongue of the people, indicated that we were in an English-speaking country. Pretty children with swarthy complexions and pearly teeth were selling branches of orange-tree upon which were ripe fruit of the past, and the fragrant blossom of the present year.

But soon we were away into the desert; the palm tree, the banana, the Italian cypress, the live oak, pepper, and eucalyptus, giving place to cacti and eternal sand as we descended lower and lower with each revolution of the wheels, until we reached the depth of two-hundred and sixty-six feet beneath the sea-level. It may be confidently stated that at a distant byegone period this basin had been filled with the waters of the ocean, because the beach around the depression can be plainly seen, the pebbles lying in rows as though the different waterlines had been left but yesterday by the receding tide. All day, with windows closed to keep out the cutting grit, and blinds closely drawn to avoid the dazzling glare, we were whirled along the oldtime bed of the sea. We had one cause of satisfaction, and that was that our train was at last progressing eastward, which was now evidenced by the fact of our days each shortening by an hour as we met the rising sun. Mr George Crofutt in his ***New Overland Tourist and Pacific Coast Guide*** has the following elegant paragraph relating to this part of the route: "Methinks we can see the huge ships sailing over our heads and many of the leviathans of the deep, with an eye cast wistfully down upon us; then we think of Jonah, and wonder if we will come out as he did; then along comes the freebooter, Mr Shark, and appears to be taking our measure with a knowing wink of his left fin—he rises to the surface as though to get a fresh breath and a better start for a good dive, looking as hungry as a New York landlord, as enterprising as a Chicago drummer (anglice bagman), and as cheeky as some of the literary thieves who pirate information from our book without giving credit!"

This is an appropriate point for me to make my bow to Mr Crofutt and to thank him for the assistance of his useful book, without which and Messrs Appletons' invaluable ***General Guide*** I could not have directed my route so as to have seen so much without a much greater expenditure of time and money. It is doubtless to a printers' error that I am indebted for the information on the opening page of the first-named book that proceeding "on, on, westward" is going towards the Orient, but such occidental mistakes are rare in the work.

Just one more quotation anent this desert. This is from Mr. S. Nugent Town-shend, the well-known "St. Kames" of the *Field*; he says "Don't get cross about it, the great American desert must be crossed somewhere, and by this road you have no alkali, and invariably good water throughout . . . . Rest contented. . . go to sleep awhile, but be certain to wake up at Yuma for supper at six o'clock." This we did, and found a city unlike any preceding one. Americans, Spaniards, Mexicans, and Indians thronged the square about the station, the buildings around which are of one storey with flat roofs and piazzas of more or less ornate construction. We learned from reliable authority that the sun sometimes marked one hundred and thirty degrees in the shade, and that the residents (as may readily be believed) "wear as little clothing as possible, sleeping on the roofs of the houses, covered by the drapery furnished by nature—darkness" (vide Crofutt).

Being about to quit California for Arizona, just a parting word as to the climate of the southern part of the former State. All the attractions that the clear skies of Greece and Italy have had from remote times for the natives of the cloudy north are excelled by Southern California. The superiority of the climate of California over that of Italy has been mentioned by many noted travellers. Samuel Bowles says "There is a steady tone in the atmosphere like draughts of champagne." Another writer says "it is like Italy's climate except that it is not enervating." It is a common saying that no people have so much local pride as the Californians, and none are so discontented when they have to move to another state or country, much of their attachment to the land being caused by the geniality of its sky. Yuma has three hundred cloudless days in a year; Los Angeles two hundred and sixty; New York, one hundred and twenty; London, sixty.

From this point guide-books were cast to one side, the compilers, whose information had being growing more and more scanty, being quite out of their depth. The railway had only been open about twelve months, so that the inevitable latest editions which follow the track of the steam-horse, and so penetrate into the new country which its advent opens up to more primitive modes of travel, were not yet in existence or had not come into our possession.

DAY THIRTY-EIGHT.

The matutinal feeding station was Tucson (pronounced tuçon), the capital of Arizona. Here we were in the second oldest town in North America, and found ourselves called "tenderfoots," a local soubriquet for all who are not dwellers in the land. Swarthy Mexicans now mingled profusely in the crowd, and Texan *vaqueros*—the cow-boys of evil fame who herd the cattle and cause great trouble to intrepid sheriffs—sauntered about in their broad hats, red shirts, pantaloons stuffed into their boots, and big spurs.

Old Spanish names and customs were now rife, and we found from conversations by the way that here, as all over the States, the modern Americans revel in anything ancient. Old silver, old lace, and family heirlooms of all kinds are highly prized, and someone who had married a descendant of a scapegrace English lord from one of the New England States was looked up to on that account as quite the *haut ton.*

But *revenons a nos moutons.* The cars were very sparsely peopled. We had never had many passengers since leaving Madera, recent robberies of trains by desperadoes, and the unsettled state of the Indian population, having made the route temporarily unpopular. A short time previously the engineer and fireman had been killed by a gang of robbers, and the treasure in the express-van had only been saved by the heroic conduct of the passengers in driving off the marauders. Travellers had not always come off so well, even on lines in much more civilized portions of the country. The alarming and familiar cry of "hands up" had not long since been uttered by masked thieves boarding the cars at stations in the Eastern States, and panic-stricken passengers had to submit to their pockets and valises being rifled, for if anyone is seen to lower a hand to grasp a weapon or hide any valuables, by the "rule of the road" he is a dead man. It was some comfort to know that the molesting of travellers is not the chief object of these "boys," as they are play-fully termed. The "express" is the car their delicate attentions are mainly directed to, and it is only in cases of disappointment in that direction that a *divertissement* among the parlour and sleeping cars is indulged in.

A male *compagnon de voyage* asked me in some trepidation whether I was aware that there were only twenty-five persons of our gender in the train. I could only reply that in the records of recent car-robberies it appeared that the ladies, of whom we had a goodly number as body-guard, had always figured as the braver part of the company. However, we got safely and punctually through our journey. The train the following day was nineteen hours late; the reason we never learnt.

At Wilcox station were groups of soldiers and excited civilians. One of the latter bore evidence of recent fighting, and it transpired that in a scrimmage with the redskins that morning, three whites had been left dead on the field. The merits of this case we failed to ascertain, but one of the "civilized" survivors was very tipsy and honoured our car with his presence for a few miles, vociferating that he was "not killed yet!"

This day's progress was through wilderness, but something less of desert than that passed through the previous day, the chief production of nature being cacti of every shape and size. One hundred and fifty varieties are said to strew the plains, chief among which is the "boss" cactus, whose prickly column stands as high as the top of the cars.

An instance of what can be achieved where water is obtainable at a reasonable depth, and the soil is susceptible to irrigation, was furnished by a square patch within a fence which enclosed all manner of fruit trees and greenery, while all around spread the cruel yellow sand, The proprietor had evidently struck a supply of water, that could be raised at a cost low enough to render it payable, sufficient for his little "claim." His windmill (when there was wind) performed its function of working the pump of the artesian well, and trenches conveyed the welcome fluid to the roots of thirsty trees and plants.

At Lordsburg, just within the territory of New Mexico, were encamped some soldiers, and at Wilna was quite a large camp of cavalry, the officers of which visited us and requisitioned, in a friendly way, our latest newspapers. They had chased some Indians across the Mexican frontier hard by, and the troops of the sister republic had killed a hundred of the "vermin," as they were politely termed. Twenty-five wretched-looking prisoners of war we saw, but Loto, the chief of the rebel Apaches, was still at large.

DAY THIRTY-NINE.

We had entered the almost exactly square Territory of New Mexico at its south-west corner, from Arizona, and the map showed that our course would take us diagonally across the Territory until, emerging at its north-east extremity, we cut through a portion of Colorado before entering the State of Kansas.

Although we had now left the neighbourhood of the Mexican frontier, and the thick of the disturbance with the Indians who originally possessed the land (and had lately carried on a seesaw dodging business across the boundaryline between the two republics until a mutual arrangement had been come to between the two Governments as to joint action in the annihilation of the "savages") we frequently met train-loads of United States soldiery bound upon their errand of extirpation.

The first look-out to-day was upon an Indian town, the Pueblos evidently not being such wanderers as other tribes we had encountered. There were substantially-fenced enclosures filled with cattle, and some of the squaws were actually engaged in tilling patches of ground. The houses were square, with sharp edges, no windows, and with chimnies; the whole made of clay—the "adobe" buildings of ages past. One would have thought that heavy rain would wash away the structure, or considerably round off the corners; but no, many of the habitations were a hundred years old, and showed no signs of dilapidation!

During the forenoon we left our main-line train at Lamy, a station so called after the good, Roman Catholic archbishop of the see, and took a branch line which brought us by an hour's ride due north to the oldest city in North America, Santa Fé, the City of the Holy Faith.

Stranger feelings came over us on arrival here than perhaps at any other point of our pilgrimage. A railway station and modern omnibus were as incongruous here as are the steam launches upon the canals of Venice and the steam-horse shrieking under the minarets of Seraglio Point at Stamboul. At first sight it had appeared that it must be one of the dead cities of the past that we were nearing, for no signs of life were visible about the yet distant cluster of earth hovels that came in view. As we rounded a bend in the track more substantial structures of stone and of wood were disclosed, and now, as we were driven through the narrow streets, we observed that a blending of ancient and modern was tardily taking place.

Old Indian customs and modes of living were as yet rather modified than discontinued, and an air of Astec-Indian, Spanish-Mexican romance pervaded the plazza as we approached the Palace Hotel. Buildings of adobe (locally called dobey) were even to-day in course of construction, the thick walls of this tenacious clay keeping out the external cold or heat in a manner peculiarly adapted to the climate. The flat roofs, covered with the same material, bore testimony more telling still than that of the walls to its imperviousness to the deluges of rain prevailing at some seasons of the year. Two old churches are built of it, as also is the cathedral. The walls of the latter, after three centuries' existence, were being encased in a modernized structure of stone, the completion of which was, or is, to witness the demolition of the adobe, hallowed by time and the sacred rites performed within its shelter through generations of struggling Christians in this far-away outpost of their religion.

At the date of our visit not a single machine driven by steam-power had obtruded into this medieval community, excepting the locomotive which brought the cars to the depôt twice daily, even the two inevitable diurnal newspapers being printed by hand power. These racy journals provide pabulum for the population of close upon eight thousand souls, and to meet the convenience of the five thousand Spanish-speaking of these inhabitants, several columns are devoted to articles in that language.

Those houses that are built of wood, or "frame-houses" as they are called, are made with piazzas, and involve the old Spanish method of having to go out of doors to get from one room into another.

Being seven thousand feet above the sea, the rarified air had upon us the ordinary effects upon visitors from the level, such as noises in the ears, disturbance of respiration, and general exhilaration.

In the evening we went to hear a lecture by a Major somebody (every other man is a general, or has some military or Salvation Army title) upon the Rhine and the Alps. It was time to commence when we arrived at the "hall," but an audience of only two individuals showed the backward state of Santa Fé society, if their desire for information about foreign parts was any criterion. A dollar a-piece seemed rather stiff, so we declined to double the company and the receipts by our presence.

Soon, however, the door-keeper accosted us in the street while we were gazing at a seductive display of Mexican filagree silver jewellery in a shop window, and said that if we would only go back we should both hear the lecture for one dollar. By this time about a score of people—being presumably the élite of the capital of New Mexico—had assembled, and the lecturer treated his subject with a wealth of words and descriptive power that was a genuine treat, and proved himself the cosmopolitan of which our American cousins hold up to us Englishmen a much needed example.

DAY FORTY.

After washing off the accumulated dust of the desert in the singularly soft waters of Santa Fé, we jumped into the omnibus and were soon transferred to the branch train, and from it into the cars of the Atchison Topeka and Santa Fé Railroad Company at Lamy.

We were still on the same elevated table land, but trees became larger and more numerous, cattle were seen grazing upon grass that was nearer to green than any that we had seen for a thousand miles, and which would doubtless, with the rains due in the following month, assume a verdant colour and richness.

We would fain have sojourned a while at Las Vegas, where the traditional Hot Springs of the doughty red warriors of old have been taken in hand by a Boston company, who have built a splendid hotel and bath-house. The twenty-two springs, ranging up to a temperature of one hundred and forty degrees, together with the salubrious mountain air, cause this to be a favourite recruiting spot for the jaded Yankees of the Eastern States.

Settlements grew thicker, and neat white tents dotted the plains, betokening a greater prosperity than the ricketty huts and mud hovels recently passed by. Trains of waggons, with their canvas covers, were wending southward and westward, drawn by powerful mules; our track running on the same line as the old Santa Fé trail, a great highway bearing volumes of exciting stories of many a desperate and bloody struggle between honest pioneers and savage natives, and more scoundrelly white marauders, until quite recent times.

As evening drew near, the twinkling camp fires, where three or four of these "ships of the desert" were brought up in a cluster for the night, told a tale of a meal being consumed, and possibly merry hour spent over the embers before turning-in for the well-earned slumber requisite for the early start and toiling progress of the morrow.

Another kind of emigrant travelling claimed attention to-night, for at a station where we made a considerable stoppage for our engine to take water and fuel, there were the cars of an emigrant railway train, shunted by sections into different sidings. A daily train of this kind is run upon both the northern and southern routes across the Continent, the time by the latter being nine days from Kansas City to San Francisco, as against the five days taken by the express. Each car is a complete house upon wheels, and the accommodation will compare with that of the palace cars, as that of the steerage of a first-class Atlantic steam-ship with the luxuries of the saloon.

Sunset was succeeded by a tremendous hail storm; and heavy masses of cloud, illuminated by bright flashes of lightning every instant, begat fears of a tempestuous night. However, as darkness deepened, the stars appeared bright and clear overhead in the streak of sky visible from the depth of the Raton Pass; and peak after peak of snow-clad "Rockies" occasionally appeared, like spires against the heavens, as our locomotive, assisted by another powerful monster pushing behind, dragged us upwards towards the Raton tunnel, where, deep in the bowels of the everlasting hills—the grand old Rocky Mountains—we commenced our downward grade into the State of Colorado.

DAY FORTY-ONE.

We had cut off the south-east corner of Colorado in the night, and passed the old town of Trinidad in the darkness, and early morning disclosed La Junta, where several of our passengers left us for the branch line leading into the heart of the Centennial State, whose mining and agricultural successes combine with its wild and attractive scenery to draw visitors and permanent inhabitants. We had left the region of "Territories" and entered again into full blown "States." Colorado arrived at that dignity in the year of the attainment of the centenary of the United States, when the great exhibition was held at Philadelphia—hence its complimentary title. While such members of the Union as New Mexico and Utah are in the embryo condition of territories, their "representatives" are appointed for them by the Central Government, and sit in the House of Representatives at Washington, but have no votes. This arrangement might commend itself to our British Parliament as a desirable one to apply to certain districts of Ireland, until their good behaviour again warranted their readmission to electoral privileges.

While upon the subject of the respective parliamentary institutions of the British Empire and the American Republic, it may be noted that the complaints sometimes heard of the numerical weight of lawyers in our House of Commons, has very little cause compared with the number of members of the legal profession who take part in making the laws which they have to administer in the country of Uncle Sam. There are fifty-five lawyers amongst the seventy-six Senators; and of the two hundred and ninety three members of Congress, no less than a hundred and seventy-seven—nearly three-fifths of the whole—are of the same fraternity.

At eight o'clock in the forenoon we were fairly into the State of Kansas, and passed through the middle of it during the ensuing day and night, following the flat banks of the here broad and sluggish Arkansas river—in some places reaching a width of as much as forty miles.

Hundreds of horses now alternated with the countless numbers of cattle and sheep feeding upon the vast flats of rich grazing land. Again extensive irrigation works were observed, and eastern progress opened out a country of higher and higher cultivation. Distinct boundaries of farms could be traced, and the dividing of tracts of land by fences of wire and sawn wood instead of the rough landmarks of the further west betokened a return towards more populous regions.

Farmers have grown immensely wealthy in this productive State; in fact its boast of being the greatest agricultural state in the Union would seem to have good foundation, its progress and development being without parallel even in this go-ahead country. Next to Massachusetts it may also be looked up to in point of intellectual distinction, for men and women of culture and progressive ideas have located themselves here on arrival from other countries, finding congenial minds and homes; and Kansas ranks as a leader among the States where liberty of thought and action are concerned.

Sturdy Scottish-bred people abound and British enterprise has added largely to the successful cattle raising and corn growing industries of the district. There is a thriving British Association whose head-quarters is at the Clifton Hotel, Florence, where the committee meet for business and social purposes on the first Saturday in every month, and hospitality and information are cheerfully accorded to fellow-countrymen passing through.

There is plenty of sport to be had, McPherson Lake containing fabulous quantities of wild fowl: grouse, quail, and prairie-duck being as plentiful as the most rapacious slaughterer of things with wings could possibly desire.

DAY FORTY-TWO.

All hands were aroused at four o'clock in the morning to prepare for going off the cars at Kansas City at five. Waving corn fields and rich pastures now met the eye, and in place of the young, artificially-watered trees that had been planted about the new houses on the level land at the western part of the State, we now had old woods of oak and other trees. In many places, however, these had been cleared away, and the stumps were visible among the green ears of wheat. For the first time for thousands of miles the railway was once more in places fenced in. Even in the most populous parts of America this is by no means a matter of course, and the immense slaughter at crossings (reported for the year 1880 as twenty-seven hundred persons) is to a great extent accounted for by the fact that the whole network of railroads is one huge "level crossing."

Kansas City (which, by the way, is not in the State of that name, but just within the borders of Missouri) is one of the most striking examples of quick growth in a quick-growing nation. Where, a very few years since, the "untutored savage" was being driven backward by the ever-encroaching Anglo-Saxon, a handsome city of sixty thousand inhabitants now stands; and its solid and graceful railway station, its public buildings and churches, would do credit to a town twice its size. True, the central and western cities have had an advantage over those on the Atlantic seaboard, inasmuch as they were laid out and their sanitary arrangements planned at a time when modern ideas in these respects had taken root; and the municipal authorities of New York and Philadelphia might do worse than take a picnic to St. Louis and Kansas City and return home to act upon some of the lessons in road-making and kindred matters to be learnt there.

After a stroll through the principal streets we took the Chicago, Burlington, and Quincey Railroad, one of the four direct lines between the cities of Kansas and Chicago, and crossed the Missouri by a bridge of over a quarter of a mile in length.

It was more to our advantage to be travelling in these regions in the year of grace, 1882, than in the dark ages of 1881, for twice during that year was the neighbourhood the scene of train-wrecking by the notorious robbers Jesse James and his gang, who for twenty years had been outlawed, but remained at large. Only fifteen days before our visit had Jesse James been killed, and his body handed over to the authorities by a "pal," Robert Ford, in consideration of ten thousand dollars and a free pardon. This same Ford had been lionized at the theatres of Chicago but a few nights before, and this morning we saw him on the platform at Kansas in the company of the sheriff, being on his trial for a murder to which the amnesty did not extend. Hopes were entertained that he would be hung for it, but it seemed more likely that it would be brought in "murder of the second degree," as American juries are loath to cause the death penalty to be put in force. The brother, Frank James, and other of the "boys" were yet uncaught, although some of their associates had surrendered with Ford, undertaking to assist in the capture of the remainder of the murdering and thieving pests.

The day after our seeing Ford he was sentenced to be hanged, on which day (19th of May) he received from the Governor of Missouri an unconditional pardon. ***Harper's Monthly Magazine*** for October, 1882, in a foot-note to an article on Railways in Mexico, gives an interesting epitome of the doings of the Jameses—Jesse being credited at the age of thirty-seven with one hundred and twenty-five lives to his own hand. The only material difference between *Harper's* account of the sequel and that heard by us on the spot, is that the former states that Ford's arrest and trial were at the instance of Mrs. James, "for murder"; but, although the inference is that the murder of her husband is meant, the "note" is capable of a reading compatible with our information. The instructive article mentioned contains the following: "There have been more train robberies perpetrated, and property of greater value taken by highwaymen in the United States during the past six years, than in Mexico, with every allowance for the difference in the territorial area of the two countries."

The long immunity of the James Brothers and their co-rascals, and the unsatisfactory ending likely to ensue, add little to the credit or possible future efficiency of the criminal administration of what may be called the Home States. Farther away, the sense of self-preservation of orderly citizens occasionally steps in, and Judge Lynch supplements the puny efforts of ordinary law. Down about Santa Fé we saw a report in a newspaper that a notorious Charlie somebody had killed "one too many," and being again in custody would likely "stretch hemp" *this* time, either at the hands of the sheriff or some other friends of order. At another place a gaol had been broken into, and a wretch, who there was some fear might get off, was summarily disposed of from a neighbouring tree, to the vindication of the public conscience and saving to the state exchequer.

As a specimen of what names of places may get to—the Saint Joseph of this neighbourhood has got to St. Joe, and then the "e" has got knocked off, and you see railway trucks with the inscription "Hannibal and St. Jo R. R." upon them. Finally the "St." has gone by the board, and the city rejoices in the curt appellation of Jo.

The Knights of Pythias, of the Ancient Order of Oddfellows, had been holding high carnival at Leavenworth, and were to-day returning home. Prizes of many dollars had been given for the best "drill," and that fact and their military-looking uniform, led to the supposition that the friendly societies hereabouts go in for calisthenics. The get-up was very imposing, being a dark blue tunic with white belt, and black cocked hat with white plumes.

We crossed the broad Mississippi in Illinois about a hundred miles above St. Louis, and spent a few hours in the State capital, Quincey, a prosperous city built of stone and brick.

Once more on board the cars, to while away the evening, I bought a book, *Among the Americans* (there is always a merchant in the train with the newest books and all manner of goods), a Chicago edition of a work by Mr George Jacob Holyoake—author of publications called *The Reasoner*, the aim of which is to prove that revealed religion is all humbug, and *A Religion which gives Heaven no trouble*, a book forming one of the "People's Popular Library," in such company as *The Law of Population,* by Mrs. Besant, and the *Impeachment of the House of Brunswick,* by C. Bradlaugh. It was edifying to read how he was fed with fruit from off a church altar; how the pulpits of popular preachers were placed at his disposal; how great "thinkers" came thousands of miles to see him; and how the big Beecher himself, seeing Mr. H. in the congregation, exhibited "a masterpiece of facility of resource," by introducing "as an inseparable part of narration" the following reverent and becoming assertion—"The third subject upon which Christ would have spoken, foreseeing as He must have done the future needs of society, would have been co-operation" (!) The quotations are from Mr Holyoake's book, and co-operation is his twin panacea (with the teaching of The Reasoner) for the troubles of modern man. We had seen in the Mormon cities the wonderful sign-boards over "the stores"—ZION'S CO-OPERATIVE STORES: HOLINESS TO THE LORD—with a cute looking eye (the "eye to business" doubtless) depicted in the centre. This would make a good motto and trade-mark for the author of the atheistical works and preacher from Christian pulpits. At this time of day scarcely anyone will deny to Mr Holyoake the right to his opinions, and their possible righteousness; but it shows an extraordinary "breadth" of American "religions" that the writer of the books mentioned above (which I have read) should be able to record—"I was asked in the morning to meet the teachers of the Sunday School (Wesleyan) and make a little speech to them. Afterwards I was asked to attend the Sunday Schools and make another speech to the pupils. This constantly occurred to me in other churches; the object was to enable the children to hear and see the stranger who had come amongst them."

It must have been very delightful to be breakfasted, receptioned, fêted, and interviewed as is feelingly and gratefully described; the bliss of it could only be approached by that of another occupier of rostrums, the Rev. Newman Hall, who in *About America,* tells us how he frequently found, upon presenting himself at the dread cashier's-desk of the hotels that it had been "made all right" by some admiring friends. Alas! such good fortune was not for us; no luscious grapes of altar-offerings were ours, and our charges (we never could get a bill) were extracted from us by an ungrateful nation, to the uttermost cent.

A Chicago newspaper, bought (by one of those coincidences inaptly termed rare) at the same time as the above-named books, stated that "one hundred pounds had been voted by Mr Gladstone's Government to Mr. G. J. Holyoake for the pur-

pose of reporting as to the Emigration of British operatives to the United States."
Evidently the "reasoning" author and his patron statesmen are ***en rapport*** upon
more subjects than one, for in the work above referred to, the former declares that
"the English people regarded the Zulu and Afghan invasions as the last wars of the
Pentateuch." Possibly he will be prepared to assert that his countrymen look upon
the Egyptian "invasion" as the commencement of the millennium.

While extolling those institutions of the Great Republic which he idolized, he
comes across the awkward subject of free trade. The way in which congregations
hung upon his lips must have given him golden opportunities of impressing upon
them, what he asserts, that "we see free trade to be as much to their interest as to
ours." Uncle Sam is too old a bird to be caught with such "chaff"; and it betokens
an inclination to say smooth things and avoid unpleasant topics, instead of a manly
boldness in pointing out the bad as well as the good, when we read—"Although a
partizan of free trade, I elected never to allude to it, having discerned before I went
that the best advocacy of free trade in America is to say nothing about it, Americans
being apt to believe that when an Englishman recommends it to' them he does so
because it is a national interest of his own."

Copious extracts are given from speeches by orators espousing the principles
professed by the author of the book, some of which speeches must make them
and him feel very foolish in the light of events which have since transpired: e.g.—
"These forty millions of people have at last achieved what no race, no nation, no
age, hitherto succeeded in doing. We have founded a Republic on the infinite suffrage of the millions. We have that serene faith in God that it is safe to trust a
man with the rights He gave him. . . . Our fathers announced this sublime, and,
as it seemed then, foolhardy declaration, that God intended all men to be free and
equal—***all*** men, without restriction, without limit." This was spoken in Boston
by Mr Wendell Phillips. How nice it reads alongside of a paragraph in the newspaper already quoted—"Discriminations against colour are becoming alarmingly
frequent. A coloured colonel was refused quarters at the Revere Hotel ***in Boston***
and a coloured clergyman was denied the privilege of sitting down to dinner at the
regular table on a Hudson river steamboat."

Theories as to equality of races and nations are all very fine, but let our friends
practise first and boast afterwards. The treatment of the Indians, the continued

refusal of the rights of citizenship to immigrants from China, together with the legislative interference with their freedom to come in, are only instances among many that the liberty of this vaunted Republic is to a very great extent liberty in name only.

Since Columbus unceremoneously took possession of the land of the copper-coloured natives in the name of Spain, it is said that five hundred millions of dollars scarcely covers the cost in money, not to reckon the lives, with which have been attempted the solution of the problem, what to do with the Indians; and the methods employed do not yet point to the simple solution, "treat him like a white man."

The Chinese—diligent, faithful, peace-loving people—who with pick and shovel have built railroads, tilled fields, and worked coal pits to the benefit of the Americans, are thrifty, and although, as I have pointed out, not eligible in the generous scope of United States law to become citizens, have paid an enormous amount of taxes to help to support the Government of the country. True, they have objectionable habits, and special vices; and so have the immigrants from other countries, who, however, are allowed to have votes and can coerce those dependent upon them for political support to commit the nation to the short-sighted policy of closing up a source of labour-supply that conflicts with the interest of the trades-unionist and his "leaders."

Strikes are getting to be very frequent, and to be truly American they have, of course, to be on an enormous scale. The protracted struggles between capital and labour in two great fields of the coal and iron industries during the present year of 1882, have caused serious interference to commerce, and have considerably opened the eyes of thoughtful citizens as to what things may come to if free trade in labour is to be prevented by Acts of Congress.

DAY FORTY-THREE.

The approach to Chicago by rail is similar to that of many large commercial towns in England. Here and there are palatial residences, and well-treed suburbs and level roads border the railway. Nearer to the end of our ride, warehouses, distant masts of shipping, and high grain elevators crowded the view, there being every evidence that we were indeed entering a mighty mercantile city; and so it proved to be, for of all the inhabited places of the earth affording reminders of Jonah's gourd, Chicago is the most striking.

Like many places of older growth, she has benefited in architectural and sanitary respects by what was a dire disaster at the time—a great conflagration. Here is a veritable Phoenix begotten of the ashes. The structures destroyed by the 1871 fire have been replaced by buildings that look to be everlasting, and the grand thoroughfares have the roadways paved with wooden blocks as in our own towns, and the sidewalks were, at the time of our going through, having their wooden planking rapidly superseded by flagging, the like of which could not be found in the world. Miles of it were already laid in State Street and the other magnificent streets parallel with, and intersecting at right angles, that splendid artery of traffic—huge blocks of stone, twelve feet by ten, and a foot thick, securely set, and needing no curbstone.

The number and size of good shops is not equalled in the States. A book depôt which we patronised was a perfect library, and museum of books; its systematic arrangement and the scholastic attainments of the male and female attendants being nothing less than wonderful. It would have taken days to go through its well-contrived stands upon the ground floor and in the numerous galleries.

The situation of Chicago is undoubtedly a super-advantage to it, and, with the exception that it is not one of the direct receiving ports of immigrants from across the seas, it has all the elements of a capital in a higher degree than New York, and will one day run her close in being practically the metropolis.

Its name is more mouth-filling than those of most of the cities in the States, the inhabitants giving each syllable its full expression—***Shick-ar-go.*** You would as soon give Gloucester, Leicester, etc., the sounding of all their letters as you would most of the United States cities. You say Washn'n, Boss'n, Bolt'mor, Nu Orl'ns, and so forth; but Chicago, like San Francisco, must have the dignity of every syllable being fully sounded.

The "dummy" cars which we met with in San Francisco, used principally for the hills, were in Chicago in general use on the flat, and trains of three cars each went noiselessly along the tramways with the greatest ease. (The word noiselessly applies to the motion only, for a bell was sounded when required to give warning of approach.)

The public-houses had some curious signs—"Pass If You Can," and "Grand Opening," being noticeable. The numbering of the houses was appaling—"George Ossley, 4444, Stockyard Street" suggesting that the shortest way to give the number would be "four fours."

A drive to Lincoln Park took us past the harbour works, and along the shores of Lake Michigan. Quite large steam and sailing vessels were visible, the sheet of water being nearly four hundred miles long and a hundred miles across, and an extensive trade being carried on between its ports and those of the chain of great lakes and rivers extending away to the ocean itself. Piers and lighthouses are built, and the waves lave a beach of white sand and shingle, just as on the borders of a boundless sea. A good slice of the foreshore has been reclaimed, and the promenades and drives are rendered more enjoyable by their contiguity to the water.

The water of the lake is used unfiltered by the inhabitants. The waterworks are of ornate construction and of ingenious contrivance, but their function is simply the pumping and distributing of the indispensible fluid. To avoid the impurities of the shore a tower has been placed two miles out, where the water is drawn into a culvert laid along the bottom of the lake. Even with this precaution, in times of heavy flood the filth from inland is carried out and causes a temporary fouling of the supply. The small Chicago river was formerly contributory to this fouling, and was also a source of danger to the health of the city, being nearly on a level with the lake, and almost stagnant. It was found, however, that by cutting a canal thirty miles in length a useful water highway could be opened out, and that the waters of the trouble some Chicago would then have a fall towards the Illinois river and thence into the Mississippi. How the inland districts liked this incursion of the sewage of a large community we did not hear, but learnt that endeavours were being made by those interested in Chicago, to have the canal made larger at national expense, under the pretext that it would prove a valuable means of communication between the Mississippi and the northern lakes in case of war.

There are seven public parks, the trees in which are of a goodly size for a mushroom city; and the landscape gardening displayed is a perfect marvel. At the time of our visit the tulip was the flower of the day, and a gorgeous display there was.

Beautifully smooth roadways are kept up, with notices prominent—"This road is reserved for fast driving." If this had been supplemented by an announcement that drivers who proceeded at such, a rate that they and their horses and vehicles could not be seen would be prosecuted, then I might have been able to describe what took place in that paradise of Jehus. The road for "slow" driving was at a lower level than, and parallel with, the other; and we poor mortals who were "by the hour" felt and heard, rather than saw, the flashing past of the stream of rapid ones. We persuaded our driver to urge his animal to a speed a little more from a stand-still, and then we could just catch a glimpse of the whirling wheels and light spider forms of the carriages, the animated faces and outstretched arms of the handlers of the "lines," and the elevated heads and reaching strides of the "steppers;" until the sight became almost as exciting to us as to the charioteers and fiery steeds themselves.

DAY FORTY-FOUR.

It would be impossible here to enter into descriptions of all the public buildings of Chicago, but it may be mentioned that the City Hall is reckoned the third finest in the country—the Capitol at Washington and the State House at Albany ranking before it. Thirteen swivel bridges, revolving on piers in the middle of the river, connect the principal streets, and are opened and shut with great ease and rapidity by hydraulic machinery.

Michigan Avenue and other splendid ***boulevards*** are lined for miles with hand-some stone residences and churches. The trees and strips of sward are well attended to and watered; and, with the flower gardens attached to almost every house and public institution away from the business centres, leave a very agreeable reminiscence with visitors.

In the afternoon we left by the Michigan Central Railroad to perform the remainder of our United States travel, to Detroit; where, crossing the river of that name, the train enters Canada.

Before stepping again upon British soil, a subject that had often been approached in my note book—the remarks as often being erased—must at length occupy a few lines, viz., the American women. They are highly educated, for their respective stations in life, and are fully able to take care of themselves. The middle classes have more of book learning than the upper ten thousand in England. We heard discus-

sions upon the binomial theory, the nebular hypothesis, and the use of the euphon-
ic vowel in various languages, by females carrying their own babies; and travelled
with ladies returning from Conferences, Conventions, and the like, whose animated
conversation disclosed their thorough mastery alike of the matters in hand and of
the mild male members who accompanied them. To converse with one of them was
a genuine pleasure—as an intellectual treat. One could admire them, revere them:
nay, almost worship them: but *love* them, never. We asked ourselves how they
ever did get men to love them, excepting their own fathers and brothers. Practical,
passionless creatures; they seemed to constitute a third sex. Where were the girls?
We never saw one. We did meet with young ladies of twelve and thirteen, with
jewel-laden fingers, and with vocabularies of ponderous dictionary words; but, like
their mothers and elder sisters, they were such superior beings that one longed for
a *lassie* that was not so very clever—one who had something yet unlearnt, that she
could ask a fellow to tell her about. Even the shallower minded, dressed-to-death,
ladies of New York, have a tremendous-share of "gumption"; and in the energy they
throw into their ravishing toilets make up for their never walking a yard when they
can get into a carriage. They lack "temperament"; and, although as a rule tall and of
good gait, "their physique is not generous, not abundant," as an American author
expresses it.

At home we have kindly ladies of all ages up to four score and over, who, if
they do know as-much or more than men, are as merciful as their position is strong,
and let man, poor fellow, feel that after all he is lord of creation. But not so in the
United States. One felt a depressing sense of inferiority, and the male population
there appeared to be under the same cloud.

A tribute must be paid to the influence of New England Puritanism to the
remotest corner of the States. Its leven spreads everywhere. The Sabbath as a rule
is better observed than in any other country but Scotland, and wherever you go
there is sure to be within a distance relatively short, according to the density of the
population, some godly man "from Boston" who as a minister, or school-master, is
looked up to and has an ennobling influence even in the roughest quarters.

True there are very many dark places of iniquity, but had not the cloak of the
Pilgrim Fathers fallen upon many and worthy successors the spiritual and moral
condition of the country would have been a sorry one indeed.

As to the resources of the Union, that is a subject a hurried treatment of which might be misleading, but as a matter of history it may be stated that in April, 1882, one hundred and eight thousand immigrants from Europe arrived at New York alone. The arrival of the population of a large city every month, with mouths to be fed, is a serious matter. The mining districts absorb many, and the food-producing north sends her wheat, poultry, vegetables, etc., to many newly settled districts, as well as to some southern States, where cotton is grown to the exclusion of foodstuffs sufficient for the population. The fact that a season has already occurred when potatoes and other edibles were freely imported from Europe, and the usual immense export of provisions to England almost entirely ceased for months, taken in connexion with the rapid pouring-in of inhabitants, may well cause anxious attention to be directed to the trade statistics of the next few years.

Another matter for thought is that there are very few young men learning trades in the States. The trades-unions render apprenticeship unworkable, and the supply of craftsmen has been, so far, kept up from abroad. The mechanics who cross the Atlantic are of Europe's best; and; untrammelled by oldfashioned fetters, their dexterity, individuality, and energy find congenial conditions in a new country, their development producing the wonders of scientific mechanism in which America is giving us the go-by.

DAY FORTY-FIVE.

A quiet Sunday at the Clifton House Hotel on the Canadian side of the Falls of Niagara, gave us an opportunity of taking in the ***tout ensemble*** of the world-famed cataracts. Our first impression was that there was comparatively very little noise, and that the masses of falling water were not so very enormous after all, but as hour after hour we gazed out of our window, or strolled along towards the Horse Shoe Fall, the thing grew upon us, and its mighty magnificence became known to our senses.

In the evening we formed part of the congregation at a little sanctuary of the Church of England—Christ Church—and heard a sermon. touching upon the state of things in Ireland preached by a stalwart Irish clergyman, whose weighty admonitions would never reach the subscribers to the baneful societies whose; existence and actions he contemned.

DAY FORTY-SIX.

The big waterworks were still at it: there was the American Fall, on the other side of the river, just opposite our balcony, thundering away the same as yesterday; and casting our eyes to the right we observed the Canadian, or Horse Shoe Fall, still in the full fling of business, not showing the least signs of an early suspension of operations.

Having a week's work to crowd into a day, we took an early advantage of daylight and crossed the Suspension Bridge to the American side.

The bridge has but one carriage way, so that two vehicles cannot pass. It is much longer than its sister structure at Clifton, in England, but is not nearly so high above the water. For grace and lightness it is unsurpassed, and we obtained favourable views of both falls in crossing it. Later on we ascended one of its towers by the elevator within, the extra hundred and twenty feet altitude giving a corresponding extension of the prospect.

Sight-seeing by machinery is now one of the features of travel, and very soon doubtless the Rigi railway and the Niagara elevators will be followed by a "lift" that will drop stage and passengers right down into the Yosemite valley, and tethered balloons that will admit of the crater of Vesuvius being safely viewed without the unpleasantness of being carried to the summit upon the crossed arms of two odourous bearers.

The absence of pedlars, advertisements, and other kindred defilements which we expected to find was gratifying. Possibly the notoriety that the "the falls" obtained as a grand spot of nature particularly disfigured by greed of Mammon, had led the authorities to cause the evil to be minimized. There was no lack, however, of devices for extracting coin from visitors for proffered services of guides, rentage for a few moments' occupancy of points of vantage, and for articles of *vertu* made by Indians and otherwise.

At the same time it must be admitted that the four miles on each side of the river, from the beginning of the Rapids towards Lake Erie, to the Whirlpool away below the railway bridge; have been well taken in hand and every point made and kept up in a condition favourable to the pleasure and comfort of the multitudinous visitors. Pity it is that such a locality should not be state-endowed by the Americans on the one side and the Canadians on the other, for it is very irritating to be met every few minutes, in response to the enquiry "How much for two," with the answer "*Whan* dollar" given with as much indifference as is thrown into the reply of a collector of Thames steamboat fares "*Two* pence."

The surroundings generally were more gratifying (because more unexpected) than the falls proper. The easy access to, and rustic beauty of, the islets and rocks in the very middle of the falling masses of water, both above and below; were unlooked for and delightful. The number of bridges suspended from island to island, or supported upon bits of rock in mid-stream, was as wonderful as their indestructibility and that of the shores which withstood the unceasing washing of the flood hurled against them.

The American Fall is separated from the Horse Shoe Fall by Goat Island with its satellites Luna Island (which is on the edge, and cuts off a strip of water sometimes called the Centre Fall), and the Three Sisters, which are behind. We viewed the American Fall, at both corners, from above—the platforms quite overhanging the cataract—and from below, but declined to go into the Cave of the Winds underneath the glassy sheet. At the Canadian side we went to the upper edge of the Horse Shoe. This fall we found to justify its name more than we had anticipated. It is not merely a semi-circle, but a deeply indented curve, the ledge of rock over which the river precipitates itself not having worn away so much next the shores as towards the centre of the stream. A recent falling away of a piece of rock had interfered with the symmetry of the "shoe": another such a wearing-away, and future generations may have to find another name for the fall—possibly founded upon its resemblance to the letter V. Even the apparently straight American Fall (when seen from across the river), falls back considerably in the middle when observed from close to and end on.

The best view of the whole, taking in both falls, the islands, and rapids, is from a slightly-built bridge from Goat Island to where the Terrapin Tower (familiar in pictures) stood until removed, as being considered unsafe. Here we stood, in the midst of the drenching spray; far beneath us was the seething cauldron; while from up the river the coming waters rushed, as "rapids," like angry waves of the sea, intent upon sweeping away our tottering foothold, and dashing it and us into the roaring abyss below!

A drive up stream along the Canadian shore still further disclosed the grandeur of these rapids. The road formerly took a turn inland, and the traveller lost sight of the river during a good part of the journey to the farthest point of exploration—the Burning Spring; but a recently constructed series of picturesque bridges carried us from the shore to Cedar Island, from there to the mainland again, and once more across the impetuous current to the Clark Hill Islands, whence we crossed the final suspension bridge to the pretty cottage on the river bank, enclosing the famous spring. The sight from the verandah of the cottage was of far more importance than the natural phenomenon within. The hurrying waters leapt from ledge to ledge of the shelving river-bed, forming series of cascades and long lines of angry foam. Here and there were trunks of large trees and portions of rafts of hewn timber, which had broken away from the upper river near to Lake Erie, and were now perched in fantastic positions upon rocks in the midst of the rapids—looking like the ribs of vessels that had been wrecked upon ocean-beaten reefs—ready to be sent over the falls when dislodged from their holding-places by the next increment to the flood. The quantity of wood in sight in this manner was astonishing, and it seemed wonderful how the slender wooden bridges and the slight embankments protecting the edges of the islands and roadways were not destroyed by the torrent-borne débris. The fast rushing of visible miles of broken water had a fascinating effect: at one point it passed our feet at the rate of twenty-seven miles an hour; a little to the right it came on at thirty-three; and, passing down from us to the left, took an extra plunge at a speed of forty miles per hour!

The spring that was the last of the show places at this side of the water was made to come into a well in the centre of a room, and a cone which collected the vapour emerging from its bubbling volume culminated in a burner that gave forth a flame like coal gas. It was stated to be sulphurated hydrogen gas, and when the collector was removed from the spring the flame continued at the burner for twenty minutes, the gas on the surface of the water forming an ***ignisfatuus*** that would presumably go on for ever if allowed its natural course.

About two miles below the falls the river narrows, the consequence being that the stream (which is so marvellously still at the foot of the falls that ferry-boats regularly traverse it) becomes turbulently rapid, the commotion terminating, at a right-angle bend, in a whirlpool. Here the water, encountering the opposing bank, turns back again, but after running parallel with the down stream for a few yards in the reverse direction, suddenly dips under the surface-current at a sharp angle, and having thus formed a loop, comes up beyond and meanders away quietly through a pretty but somewhat commonplace gorge to Lake Ontario.

The so-called "perpendicular railroad" from the top of the cliff to the edge of the whirlpool (four hundred feet down the incline) was a curiosity to us, no motive-power being visible. We were conducted to the rear of the little break-cabin at the summit and saw a wheel over which was suspended an endless chain of buckets after the manner of a dredger. There were a hundred and sixty-eight of these buckets, which hung down into a cleft of the rock. There were always fifty-four of them full of water, while a like number were coming up empty. The supply came from a little trickling rill that filled one bucket at a time. Five persons could be drawn up by this simple contrivance—the invention of the proprietor. The Whirlpool Cottage must be a melancholy place to live at, for the numerous bodies of suicides and persons drowned by accident at, and for miles above, the falls, all come to the surface at this spot, and gyrate upon the inland Charybdis until brought to the shore.

DAY FORTY-SEVEN.

After a ride of three hours by rail, having passed the town of Hamilton about noon, we arrived at Toronto, a well-built city of nearly a hundred thousand inhabitants. One of its features is a long strip of an island lying out in the lake (Ontario) about two miles from the shore, where many of the Torontonians reside during the summer, leading a kind of "camping out" life. The lake-side situation of Toronto is effective, and the country around is highly cultivated and picturesque. An utter absence of paving or macadam causes all the streets to be perfect bogs in wet weather, and the wooden sidewalks, although cleanly, and good to walk upon where not worn into holes, are not consistent with the pretensions of the architecture.

A prominent part of the town is spoken of as the "Four Ations." This appellation was explained to us by the fact of the corner buildings being respectively the Government House, Upper Canada College, a Scottish Presbyterian Church, and—a public house; some local wag having immortalized them as Legislation, Education, Salvation, and D——ation. He must have, been an irreverent and rabid teetotaler, or else he would have managed short of having recourse to profane language by making the fourth word Intoxication, or, better still, *Liquidation.*

We did not see more than the solid brick exterior of the educational institution mentioned; but were shown over the University of Toronto, a pleasing gray rubble building of true Norman architecture with bold facings of a lighter coloured stone, forming three sides of a quadrangle. The natural history museum and handsome well-stocked library were exceedingly well arranged. In the lecture hall we saw from the gallery some dozens of male students—and one female—grinding away at formidable-looking "papers," which were handed in as fast as completed to the examiners sitting stern and awe-inspiring on the dais at the farther end of the room.

The University building is surrounded by a well-wooded park which contains an interesting monument erected by the students to their fellow volunteers who fell in repelling the Fenian raids of 1866. It is a massive stone column surmounted by a colossal statue of Britannia, and looks very handsome surrounded as it is by sombre-hued evergreens.

Another example of pure Norman style that it would be difficult to find excelled among modern buildings in Europe, is St. Andrew's Presbyterian Church; in fact the public edifices of Toronto struck us as being decidedly above the average for a place of its size. Doubtless it will shortly mend its ways in the matter of pavements, when, with its handsome shade-trees and well laid-out plots, it will take that rank for beauty, which, as being second in population to Montreal, might be expected of it.

Two morning dailies, the *Globe* and the *Mail* respectively, represent the Liberal and Conservative sides of Dominion politics, and enjoy the position of metropolitan organs in both Upper and Lower Canada, there being no newspapers of their size and importance published in any other part of the Dominion.

An evening spent under the hospitable roof of the Toronto Club, besides being enjoyable, was very instructive; for, it being the eve of a general election, the neutral ground of a sociable institution gave a valuable opportunity to a stranger of hearing the merits and demerits of both sides, and of taking in a general impression of the politics of the day.

Toronto must not be left without mention being made of its valuable zoological collection, for, in addition to the usual menagerie of living wonders, there was a dead whale which had been rendered imperishable by being mummified in a most perfect manner. It was proved by a scientifically accurate method of computation to have lived and roamed in the ocean for upwards of four centuries, and in its present dried up state weighed ten tons.

DAY FORTY-EIGHT.

The Queen's birthday. Many happy returns of the day to her Most Gracious Majesty! Canada was en fête. They celebrate the day upon its proper date here, and celebrate it in proper style, too.

All business was suspended, bells rang, cannons were fired, bunting flew, bands played, and everybody behaved in such a manner as to have a jolly headache next morning. It was with difficulty that we travel—intent people got: through the giddy throng at the miserable railway station and procured a seat in the train; and when we did get ourselves and packages safely on boards it was an hour behind time before the loyal holiday-makers were provided; with a sufficient number of extra cars; and the festooned, evergreened, and ribbon-ornamented locomotives dragged their heavy freight of light-hearted people along the railway that skirted the lake to Kingston, where, later in the day, we took steamer on the river St. Lawrence for Montreal.

Queen's weather still favoured us as we entered that reach of the noble river, called the Lake of the Thousand Islands. For forty miles we threaded these seventeen hundred (exact official figures 1692) "islands," passing so near to many of them that a biscuit could be thrown across into the water beyond. It will thus be seen that some are but little patches; but all bear luxuriant vegetation; and some are many miles in extent. The silvery streaks and broader channels of water form labyrinths which are a paradise for waterfowl, and for their natural enemy—the sportsman.

Monotonously similar white lighthouses mark out the deep water channel, and, if not picturesquely diverse in their own construction, serve to agreeably diversify the sameness of land and water and greenery and rock through which the traveller sails along.

Among splendid villas at Alexandra Bay was one which we delighted to honour—the seat of Mr Pullman; whose invention, the palace car, had added so much to the comfort of our journey.

Suddenly we came upon the open water, where the majestic river flows on of a breadth of from two to three miles; and, doubtless missing many delightful views in the darkness, we retired to our berths, where slumbers quite as delightful to us under the circumstances as any glorious prospect, prepared us for fresh delights at the rising of the morrow's orb of day.

DAY FORTY-NINE.

Before arriving at Montreal for breakfast we experienced the remarkable sensation of "shooting the rapids." Previous to the year 1840 it had been noticed that rafts of timber drifted nine miles in forty minutes, and watching their course it was determined to try it with a steamer. The bold experiment succeeded and serious accidents have been unknown. The upward voyages are performed by canals and locks, but the downward passage is made through Nature's waterway under the guidance of Indian pilots. At the time of our "shooting" the river was swollen, a circumstance which, while adding zest to the performance, was at the same time a favourable condition for safe transit, by providing a greater depth of water. It is a peculiar feeling to be going downhill by water, even while it continues to run tolerably steadily; but, as you see the ridges of white foam coming nearer, and grim rocks sticking up apparently right in your course, your heart has a tendency to come correspondingly nearer to your mouth. The engines were slowed, but the boat continued to go faster and faster. Four men were at the wheel with eyes riveted upon an island ahead which it appeared certain we must be dashed against. Our breath was held while we considered which side of the island it was possible for us to shave. A glance at the stern visage of our pilot begat confidence. He spoke not to the steersmen; nor even made the slightest visible sign to them; but his senses and their actions were in as complete accord as the eyes and hands of one man. On we went, slipping past the right hand side of the island at an ever increasing speed. On either side were protruding rocks that threatened to pierce the sides of our bark. "Surely one of them *must* rip her open as she heels over against them!" No; we were still afloat, but close under our bows was seen a ledge, over which the dark brown torrent poured and broke into foam in a manner that no doubt formed a very pretty picture from the shore, but to us novices in rapid-shooting seemed a fearful leap to take "Good heavens! the steamer is broadside on; we are—lost! we are—no, we are *over!*" or rather we were *through,* for an oblique break in the ridge—to "take" which it was necessary that our vessel at the nick of time should be put partly across the stream—had admitted us to glide safely down with the rushing flood; instead of being dashed over a foaming cascade to certain destruction; and we were at length, upon a smooth swift-flowing tide, borne quickly under Stephenson's "Victoria" tubular bridge to the quay at Montreal.

The Windsor Hotel at Montreal is one of the chief glories of the Canadians. Splendidly situated and superbly finished and furnished it is indeed a comfortable and luxurious inn for the worn traveller, arriving either from a storm-buffetted Atlantic voyage, or a continental wandering by road and rail. It is not so stupendous as some of the hotels in the States, but its appointments eclipse anything of the kind in Europe. It has all the good points of our English hotels, combined with American conveniences—even to the "tonsorial department" on the basement. Its entrance hall and "rotunda" are unique in beauty and adaptation.

The city lies on a plain, immediately to the rear of which rises a hill seven hundred feet high, which provides public park, cemeteries, and points from which to view the urban district and surrounding country. We took our first drive to this desirable elevation, so as to get the best idea of the plan of the neighbourhood. The hill is very aptly named Mount Royal (hence the name of the city). Along the river for four miles stretch the streets and buildings, reaching inland about two miles. The noble river can be discerned entering the landscape on the far-away right of the spectator, and disappearing on the extreme left towards the distant ocean. Its many islands and rapids are plainly visible, and the monstre railway bridge (nearly two miles long) looks a mere toy in the vastness of the picture.

Both sides of the St. Lawrence are here Canadian territory, but away on the southern horizon the Green Mountains of Vermont show that the American Republic there holds sway.

The mountains of St. Clair, Belleisle, and Busheville, rise against the eastern sky, and to the northward is a fertile country melting away to bleak-looking hills in the direction of Labrador. The whole of the ground for many miles, particularly along the banks of the river, is covered with habitations; which, being mostly whitewashed and standing amid plots of well cultivated land and trees, give an idea of prosperity and happiness that is everywhere evident in Canada.

Descending the easily graduated slopes of the back of the hill (or mountain, as the Montreal people call it), we went on our tour of the city. The solid grey limestone presents a display of continuous substantial masonry unequalled on the North American continent; and fountains and statues are not wanting to testify to the successful efforts of the citizens to maintain the reputation of Montreal as a model city for construction and embellishment.

About half of the population being of the old French stock, and still clinging to their original Norman patois, there is as much of the French language used as English. Many of the streets are marked Rue so and so, only; while others, as well as public notices of all kinds, are exhibited in both languages. At the French cathedral of Notre Dame we had an opportunity of seeing a large assemblage of the French Canadians, for they were gathering to the First Communion of a batch of the rising generation. The young misses were dressed in white, with veils, flowers, and gloves, all complete; as may be seen on any like occasion in the Roman Catholic towns of Europe; and the boys with white gloves and a piece of ribbon round the arm were very unattractive objects beside the silk and satin cased little queens of whom their soberly clad mothers were so conspicuously proud. We did not wait for the service, but were duly impressed by the decoration of the church; which, being entirely of blue and gold, was as lightsome as the style of architecture would admit of. To accommodate a congregation of eleven hundred people, the floor sittings were supplemented by two tiers of galleries all round, excrescences which, it may be imagined, required a good deal of "lighting up." What I never saw before in a Romish church, the whole space was covered with pews: high ones with doors, just as in an old-fashioned church at home that has escaped "restoration." This dwarfed the seeming size of the place, and gave an impression of incongruity.

The Church of the Lady of Loudres was much more a reminder of the beautiful churches of France, being a very gem of ecclesiastical structure and adornment.

A large edifice, to be called the Cathedral of St. Peter, was in course of construction near the Windsor, after the plan of St. Peter's, at Rome. Its design included five domes and twenty chapels, and it is doubtless by the time this volume is in the hands of the reader a finished and striking example of the wealth and power of Roman Catholicism in Canada.

The Episcopal Cathedral is a unique specimen of English Gothic, and is surmounted by a spire two hundred and twenty-four feet in height.

At sunset we took our places on board a comfortable and fast river steamer for Quebec, again preferring the comfortable water-travelling to the stuffy railroad cars for which we held tickets.

The evening came in very chilly as we stood upon the spacious deck bidding good-bye to kind friends whom it was unlikely we should ever see again. Well may the people have such an affection for their city and wax enthusiastic when expatiating upon its attractions, thought we, as we watched its receding cut-stone wharves, and the panorama in. the rear. The "mountain", formed a dark back-ground against the pale northern sky, and the picture was filled in by the tall spires, glittering roofs and domes, and the deep still water between us and the shore, as the sun sank grandly beneath the western horizon, laving all in a sheen of burnished gold. It was not unlike a departure from Hamburg to proceed down the Elbe for the North Sea, but the number of ships here provided not a hundredth part of the forest of masts visible in the great German river. We passed one of the huge St. Lawrence rafts of lumber on its way down to Quebec. It was an acre in extent, and was peopled by men, women and children, who had a hut upon it and were chanting their evening hymn around a cheery fire blazing away upon the raft. Severe storms sometimes sweep down upon the river and play havoc with these masses of lumber, and cause their "crews" to be drowned in the angry flood.

DAY FIFTY.

The comfort of the spacious sleeping quarters on the steam-boat cannot be described. A white, sweet, and cosy state-room was relinquished with regret as we hastened to enjoy a glorious sunrise as we neared the harbour of Quebec.

It occurred to us here to notice that in all the sleeping places we had been in, whether on board of steamers or cars, or elsewhere since we left home, the utmost cleanliness of domestic arrangements had been conspicuous. Charles Waterton, the famous naturalist, records with satisfaction that during his American travels in 1824 he only found "one bug between Buffalo and Quebec": we were proud to be able to say that that was the exact number of this interesting natural history specimen which crossed our path during the whole of our round: only ONE—but he *was* a whopper.

The river had narrowed, and on either side was bordered by high banks covered with trees, and dotted with neat cottages and clusters of larger buildings. A few scores of the most wretched ocean-going craft afloat were anchored in the stream awaiting cargoes of timber. The whole of them were barques, and most of them flying the Norwegian flag. Their build in some cases betokened that they had at one time been British property, having very likely been sold to the foreigner for an old song when Mr Plimsoll rendered it impossible for them any longer to ply as English vessels. There were nevertheless a considerable number of our own nationality among the fleet of old maritime curiosities. The tars were astir, and the smoke from the galley fires and the redolent odours as we threaded our way through them told that a savoury meal was about to preface the labours of the day. Windwill pumps were at work, keeping under the water in the holds from the everlasting leaks in the old tubs, and splintered stems showed how the ice had offered obstruction in the Gulf of St. Lawrence, where they had been more or less delayed in its relentless grip.

The north-west bank of the river assumed the form of a large tongue of land, getting higher and higher until it culminated in Cape Diamond, crowned with the vast fortifications forming the Citadel of Quebec. The fortress from the river looked like Gibraltar, a designation which we afterwards learned had often been applied to it.

Landing at the Lower Town we found ourselves in old French-looking streets, and might have been in Dieppe or Rouen; while the cries of "Voiture Monsieur" and "Vant a carriage?" showed that we were in a mongrel country as to the language. The population is nine-tenths French-Canadian, the language used in the law-courts and written and printed being the French of to-day, but the spoken "garbage" (as our intelligent and useful cab driver called it) is boasted of as not being a patois, but the polite French of the age of the colonization of Canada. There is a colour of probability about this, but doubtless the "polite" language has become somewhat corrupted. It struck us as if a colony of English descent were to be speaking in the "vulgar tongue" of the day when the Bible was translated into the Authorized Version.

The quiet dreamy life was almost stifling after the briskness of the Yankees. Quebec is the only place in North America of any pretensions that is going back in population. It contains about fifty thousand inhabitants. The neighbourhood, however, is thickly peopled with a thrifty and easily satisfied people, the three towns of Point Levi, New Liverpool, and South Quebec, on the opposite bank of the St. Lawrence, being steady-going prosperous communities.

Ascending to the Upper Town we were within the walled city, the original gates of which are being replaced by appropriate new ones. Two, the Kent Gate and Dufferin Gate, upon the sites of the ancient St. Louis and St. Patrick, were completed. Better to have kept to time-consecrated names we thought, and so did others to whom we made the observation. The king's bastion crowns the Citadel just above the residence of the Governor General, the Marquis of Lorne, which was just being prepared for the Princess Louise and his lordship; they having left Liverpool that day in the ***Sarmatian.*** The prospect is grand, being similar to that which is obtained from an unrivalled promenade a little beneath, formed by Durham Terrace and Dufferin Terrace. There can be no denying that this outlook is the finest of its kind in the world. That from the Hoe at Plymouth resembles it in many features.

The St. Charles river joins its majestic compeer at the foot of the eminence, and right across the larger stream, to the left, lies the Island of Orleans, which, for a length of twenty miles, divides its waters into reaches of lake-like silver, in which the picturesque banks are clearly reflected.

The many striking churches, nunneries, colleges, etc., and the shining roofs of many of the buildings, added to the richness of the scene. Behind the Citadel lie the historic Plains of Abraham, and here we touched the miserable column with which a grateful nation commemorates the deeds and death of gallant General Wolfe, who fell on this spot in the moment of his victory over the French General Montcalm. The monument is a comparatively new one, replacing the original which had been carried away in chippings by Vandals of tourists.

On the road to the Falls of Montmorenci we were among trees of old growth, and the cleanly villages were essentially of Normandy, even to the dogs harnessed to the heavy barrows (in one case the lazy *man* sitting upon the top of the load). It was sad to see this unthinking brutality transplanted to a new Continent. Patches of snow still lay in valleys close by the road, and could be seen not far up on the adjacent hills. We passed, embowered in foliage, a cottage where the Duke of Kent, the Queen's grandfather, once spent a summer, and, after crossing a bridge over a ravine, found our-selves at the entrance to the grounds from which the falls could be inspected. A sylvan walk brought us once more in sight of the river and its islands, and sharp to our right a fine column of water fell two hundred feet into a basin that emptied into the river by a channel a quarter of a mile in length. The placidity of the short stream below has led to the supposition that the main body of the water of the fall disappears into the bowels of the earth. This is, however, not so. The falling water does indeed pitch into a hole at the foot in a manner that might cause you to think it was going to the centre of the globe, but the stillness of the rivers close up to the foot of Niagara, and other cataracts, prove that the greater part of the descended fluid is carried away in currents beneath the surface.

Towers at either side of the top of the cliff are the remains of a suspension bridge which, prior to 1856, spanned the chasm. Its history is evidence that these pieces of "engineering" are not everlasting, and gives force to the objection that some nervous people have to trusting themselves to their frail-looking support. A carriage with three occupants was crossing it, when it gave way; and horses and all went away with the spray, and not a vestige of the equipage or its occupants was ever seen again. This incident gave strength to (if it did not originate) the blind tradition as to the bottomless cauldron, but doubtless the bodies and the shattered vehicle would not come to the surface until far on their way to the all devouring ocean.

DAY FIFTY-ONE.

We had been told to be on board of the good steamship ***Circassian*** at half-past eight sharp, as she was sure to be under weigh at nine; but one of those inevitable (one might almost say usual) delays occurred by which our actual sailing was half an hour past noon. The time was in this case not grudged by us, as the view from the buoys in the broad St. Lawrence during the bright forenoon was magnificent. No port in the world can show such a departing scene to travellers under such circumstances: the spires and roofs of Quebec—in very many instances covered with burnished tin—glittered in the sun; the busy steam ferryboats plying from shore to shore; and the crankey ice-beaten old barques that had recently arrived from Norway, England, and other countries, lying lazily at anchor, or being towed by snorting tugs from mid-stream to their loading-berths.

Three busy towns spread their populous borders along the southern bank, forty miles behind which commences the territory of the United States. Ship-building was proceeding to the extent of half-a-dozen wooden vessels in various stages of construction, some masted and almost ready for launching, and others just showing the gaunt ribs of their timbers, bare, or partially covered with planking.

As we proceeded down stream with the Island of Orleans to our left, the banks on both sides continued dotted with white houses, which occasionally formed clusters amounting to villages and towns. This continuation of thickly inhabited country for two hundred miles down was a matter of surprise. There were patches of snow remaining on the hill sides, not very high above the water, and as the afternoon wore on the temperature became anything but summer-like. The widening river was perfectly bare of any craft but our own and the lightships which now and then appeared, as did trim lighthouses perched upon rocky islets, marking the navigable channel in the watery waste of (before nightfall) twenty miles across. Hundreds of ***white*** porpoises turned their repulsive, shark-like bodies slowly over, their movements being more deliberate than those of their darker coloured brethren, and the fin not appearing during the semicircular progress common to the marine porker of all waters. Thirty miles down we noticed Grosse Island, where fleets of merchantmen have been long detained in times of serious epidemics, in the olden days, and where hundreds of gallant seamen have died and been buried beneath its patch of emerald sward. Such visitations are now rare, and this evening there was only one solitary ship lying in quarantine opposite the lonely little "health station." Six miles further down were the picturesque Crane, and Goose, and half-a-dozen other islands, where wild birds of all sizes were hovering around—their mates being engaged in the duties and pleasures of bird-parentage, this being a favourite breeding place.

On the north bank could be distinctly seen, rising majestically from the rest of the white-washed buildings forming the village of Ste. Anne de Beaupé, the noted church of that ilk, where miraculous cures are effected by the relics of the saint which are exhibited at morning mass: so, in remote nooks by New World rivers, as in the Old World vales and forests, does that faith which will remove mountains, cause bodies to be healed, and possibly souls to be benefitted, by implicit confidence in, and reliance upon, the efficacy of the medium that presents itself to the claimants for relief.

The bold promontory of Cape Tourment and the frowning peaks of Cape Rouge and Cape Gribanne intensified the closing shades of evening, and formed a fine contrast to the bright sky in which the moon presently shone forth with welcome effulgence. As her lunar majesty would attain to full illuminating power during our voyage we comforted ourselves with the reflection that we should be troubled with very little darkness—an agreeable prospect, as rumours were rife as to the prevalence of ice to be guarded against as we approached the ocean.

About midnight we touched at Rimouski, and took on board the mails and some passengers from New Brunswick and Nova Scotia; and also the latest mail-bags from Canada, which left Montreal. Quebec. &c., by rail, some hours later than those which were put on board at the commencement of our voyage.

DAY FIFTY-TWO.

The last sight we had at one time of the two shores of the grand British North American river was in the early morning, when we could dimly discern Point de Monts on the northern coast and Cape Chatte on the opposite side. The grim cold-looking land took, beyond Point de Monts, a northward turn, and we had in that direction an open sea view. Taking a south ward course, our vessel rounded the great shoulder of the Province of Quebec, and after passing between its eastern point, Cape Rosier, and the desert island of Anticosti, we were fairly in the Gulf of St. Lawrence. A biting east wind met us in the face, and showers of rain and sleet, with occasional masses of soft floating ice, presaged anything but a genial passage.

We headed for the channel between the western extremity of the island of Newfoundland, Cape Ray, and Cape Breton on the mainland of Nova Scotia; it being considered that in this unusually backward spring it was yet too early to use the ordinary summer course to the north of Newfoundland, through the Straits of Belleisle. (There is a still more northerly and shorter route, between Anticosti and Labrador, but its navigation by large ocean steamers had been discontinued; several losses of vessels having occurred among its dangerous shoals, the ill-fated steamer **North Briton,** with many lives, being one of them.)

Things were getting shaken down on board our well-appointed ship, and the two score each of male and female saloon passengers now began to group in those mysterious coteries into which the heterogenous concatenation of human units on board ship inevitably resolves itself. Divine service at ten thirty (it was Whit Sunday) brought together nearly all the first-class passengers, and many from the "intermediate" and steerage. Abbreviated Common Prayer was read by a clergyman of the Church of England. The ordinary Morning Service was judiciously shortened for the occasion, but might have been further curtailed by the omission of the Athenasian Creed. In our unconsecrated sanctuary there would have been no violation of the rubric (any more than there was by the other omissions), and the parson was secure from being brought to book by any "aggrieved parishioner"; but with that perversity so unfortunately characteristic of his cloth he read (some ill-natured persons said in an unmistakeable tone of triumph) the "creed" with the debateable clauses. His want of taste in a mixed company of all denominations and shades of opinion was responded to by nearly all present *not* responding to the affirmations that he who does not think as we think "shall without doubt perish everlastingly." I am not going to deny to my fellow Churchmen the right to repeat the words and mentally qualify them as they find compatible with their understanding of the English language and Christian charity; nor to question the reasoning by which erudite and sincere divines reconcile their obligation regarding its use with their consciences; but I do say that it is too bad that so many of the clergy should, whenever opportunity offers, do all they can to put weapons into the hands of the enemies of their Church, and to place at a disadvantage those lay champions without whose help, politically, socially, and financially, the Establishment, as such, would assuredly go to the wall.

In marked contrast to this good man's view of his duty (which, be it understood, we canvassed not in a reviling spirit, but as fellow-strivers to do good) was that of the other minister on board, a Presbyterian. In the evening he was invited to read the lesson and preach, and took for his text, "If He had not come." His sermon was a simple gospel discourse; not touching upon the doctrinal points which different workers in the vineyard find it useful or indispensable to interpret in different ways according to their several fields of labour.

Mr Holyoake and the Rev. Newman Hall in their American books regret that the religious services on board the Atlantic liners should, as a regulation, be those of the Book of Common Prayer. This is allowing their prejudices to warp their judgment; for in a congregation in which members of the Church of England or its American sister nearly always outnumber those of any other, or no, denomination, and where the captain or other layman frequently has to officiate, what more desirable arrangement than that a "liturgy of sound words" should be enjoined?

DAY FIFTY-THREE.

Soon after midnight I was awakened by a shock to the vessel, and a sound of something more than the ordinary splash of the water along her sides. There could be no mistaking that we were in contact with floes of ice, and a visit to the deck put it beyond all doubt. Patches of white spread as far as could be seen in the shower of sleet, and as the steamer's bow slowly parted the drifting masses they sparkled with stars of phosphorus, and passed away to the stern. A sailing ship was going northward, having the ice and wind with her; otherwise there was nothing in sight excepting the heaps and lumps of ice, some of which were five feet out of the water. The moon was of little service, owing to the heavy curtains of snow-laden clouds.

The captain expressing hopes that no heavier obstruction would be met with, I turned in out of the bitter blast. During the darkness the ice continued to grate past the ship, the grinding noise being varied every now and then by a concussion, as a larger obstacle than usual was encountered. The wind was dead in our teeth and so had loosened the accumulation that had settled down upon the shores of Cape Breton. Captain Smith said that on his outward passage not a particle of ice had been seen, and the *Parisian,* which we passed during the previous night, had made her voyage from Liverpool in a space of time that showed that she had met with no serious hindrance.

Great care was taken that pieces of ice should not break the propeller. When the men on the look-out saw a "snag" of dangerous size ahead the engines were slowed or stopped until the ugly customer glided past, then full speed again, for next to the importance of proceeding cautiously was that of getting out of the pack as quickly as possible. This was accomplished before breakfast-time, and during the forenoon we rounded Cape Ray, and stood in an easterly direction for the Island of St. Pierre, the souther-most of a group of French islets on the banks of Newfoundland. The wind blowing stifly from the south (the direction of the Gulf Stream) it was warmer, and although the rain ceased, only occasional glimpses of the Newfoundland coast could be had through the driving "banks" of fog.

DAY FIFTY-FOUR.

The wind being south-south-west a gentle rain served to modify the density of the fog so that we could keep on going at full speed, having, however, a very sharp look-out.

During the afternoon I espied what might have been a sail looming through the mist, but it proved to be a huge iceberg. Twenty-two more came rapidly into sight, besides numerous treacherous pieces that were just awash with the surface of the water. These customers were very bad to discern, as they had every appearance in common with the white crests of foam until close under our bows.

The ocean-roll having now begun to be felt in real earnest, our company at dinner was considerably thinned, the tables presenting the aspect of a decimated regiment after a battle. Ominous gaps occurred in the ranks, and empty chairs told of many a pitiable case of mal de mer. As the meal progressed, others who had bravely faced the soup, and perchance made a bold charge at the entrees, had to beat a more or less graceful retreat, until only those remained who were happily destined to escape the dire infliction altogether, for the motion was such as to test the most stubborn of gastronomic arrangements.

One doughty old gentleman made a grand effort to get through to dessert, but succumbed at last and joined the majority, much to the sorrow of his neighbour, who expressed commiseration which might have been most heartfelt. The reason of this deep concern eked out afterwards: the afflicted one and the disinterested commiserator occupied the same state-room.

All kinds of preventives, remedies, and contrivances, were produced to combat the squeamy malady, and it was noticeable that those who had the most "infallible" specifics were the first to become victims. The ship's doctor had very few opportunities of administering his own particular nostrum, among so many devices. A good lady who earned a small cask of pills "one to be taken every hour" was early in the hands of the stewardess; and the man who had to inhale from a pocket handkerchief the fumes from so many drops of a certain liquid was discovered in the smoke room in a comatose condition, so that the last state of that man was worse than the first.

The sun set and the moon rose without a cloud, and night closed in as we were fairly away upon the Atlantic Ocean. Bright flashes of aurora illuminated the northern sky, and as many as nine bergs, all of immense size, were in close view at one time. Thankfulness for such favourable weather and a wind directly with us filled our hearts as we retired for the night, even the sufferers from sea-sickness being cheered by the reassuring conversation of our merry, confidence-inspiring, Captain

Smith. He and his trusty officers had to look forward to an anxious night in guiding us safely through the dangers of the intricate navigation, two men being constantly on the look-out at the mast-head, in addition to those on the pilot-bridge and at the bow.

DAY FIFTY-FIVE.

The morning report was that the night had continued clear, and the ***Circassian*** had threaded her way through sixty icebergs in the first watch alone. As there were twenty within range of vision when we went on deck, and we were rarely with fewer than this number in sight during the remainder of the day, the reckoning of a fellow-passenger, that we saw in all a hundred and ninety-five, what he called floating mountains and islands of ice, would not be over the mark. The smaller pieces could be numbered by thousands. Our commander assured us that he had never fallen in with such a number of bergs, nor so large.

The day continued serene, and almost warm, in spite of the cooling effect of the refrigerating strangers; and the wind kept on blowing from the west, with a rolling sea.

This day was by far the most enjoyable I ever spent upon the ocean. All on board were in esctacies, a feeling which spread to the invalids, all but the very weakest of whom joined the throng on the deck, who, as the hours sped by, were spell-bound by the glorious procession of icy monsters. To see such a sight under such circumstances of comfort and comparative immunity from danger was an event of a life-time. The blue sea was studded with masses of white, from the size of an orange to the dimensions and shape of Heligoland. The latter was complete, even to the shelving beach at one end and the lighthouse at the other extremity. No word-picture can convey an idea of the splendid spectacle. It would require the pencil of a master artist, and how is such to obtain "sittings" from such a series of subjects as were presented to our gaze, without benumbed fingers and frozen pigments embarrassing his depicture?

The hues of walls of ice with a strong sunlight or fine moonlight upon them have a unique beauty, which, while remaining for a lifetime in the memory of the beholder, baffle all description. I have read, and been thankful for, the entrancing sentences in which graphic writers have—withal faintly—conveyed to the reader the effects of glacier scenery, but to my mind nothing on earth so defies the pen and the tongue as the colours of solid ice. The shapes are easier to deal with, and I will instance some of the most remarkable of those we saw. By moonlight we had Jedburgh Abbey, and a slice cut off Beachy Head; in these cases size and whiteness being taken into account as well as shape. It must be understood that the bulk below-water far exceeds the visible mass, and that this accounts for the ponderous steadiness of the towering blocks, the waves dashing against their base and wearing out caves just as along a coast of rocky cliffs.

In the daylight panorama we picked out the Bass Rock, upon which were two seals and a polar bear, which were declared by enthusiastic observers to move about; others, however, declared that the supposed animals were nothing more lively than knobs of the frozen mass, which, as the steamer moved on, occupied different relative positions in the field of the beholder's vision! There was a sofa upon which Hercules might have reclined to cool himself, not omitting a footstool for his huge foot to rest upon if he dropped a leg overboard in his chilly slumbers. Churches and cathedrals were numerous, and were variously christened according to fancy; some of the fair *voyageurs* uttering such ejaculations as "Oh, isn't that York Minster!" "Isn't that the image of dear old St. Albans!"

The most true of any of the representations to the eye of the writer, was a model (a hundred fold size) of one of the steep-pitched roofed farm-houses of Holstein— one of those where the farmer, his household, and live stock all dwell together beneath the big thatch which constitutes granary and curing room. This "toy" had a chimney in the middle of the roof, and the roof actually had eaves. As we passed to the end the correct angles of the gable were astonishing. These phenomena and the evenness of the roof were to be accounted for by the melting effects of the sun, the regularity of the dropping resulting therefrom, and the settling of a snowy fleece upon the slopes by reason of the warm vapour coming in contact with the frigid surface.

Some of the pilgrims from the paloeocrystal sea we viewed from a distance of many miles; others we passed within a few hundred yards, The specific gravity of the ocean around us was tested, and showed that the fresh water visitors were leaving their impression as they went melting along, for the sea was less salt than in its normal condition in these parts. At first we were to the south of the spectral procession, as it majestically rounded Cape Race; but before we left it on its way to certain destruction in the Gulf Stream, we cut right through its watery milky way, and bade adieu to the ghostly monsters as they wafted their cool farewell to us in the pale moonlight, from both north and south in our wake.

The thermometer on the evening of the thirty-first of May stood at thirty-nine degrees Fahrenheit.

DAY FIFTY-SIX.

Never a ship had more favourable conditions for crossing the Atlantic, since we left the Banks of Newfoundland. The wind, half a gale, was continuously with us; sometimes slightly from one side, sometimes the other, but invariably favourable. The spreading canvas imparted a sensation of dashing speed, but it was known to the initiated that the sails, while steadying the ship and easing the strain upon the engines, did not help much in getting her forward.

We had not a drop of water on the deck, and the day sped quickly by as if we were on a pleasant yachting cruise.

DAY FIFTY-SEVEN.

Captain Smith—Lieutenant Smith of the Royal Naval Reserve—devised all kinds of amusements, in which nearly all of us joined enthusiastically. There were football, quoits, and shuffle-board, on deck; draughts, cards, and rehearsals for grand concert, below. Two German violinists were imported from the steerage, and dancing went forward on the quarter-deck from breakfast until bed-time. A troupe of Christy minstrels from the forecastle gave a matinée *that was highly appreciated; but the* piece de resistance was the Drill of the Mulligan Guards, where a colonel (the bos'n's mate) on a spirited donkey—a wonderful piece of anatomy, into the formation of which a tarpauline, the cook's boy, and some teazed hemp largely entered—put the corps through a variety of evolutions that would have done credit to the most practised of clowns. The masks, and the decayed uniform of various regiments imparted a highly ludicrous aspect to the bold guard.

DAY FIFTY-EIGHT.

Placards announcing that the "*Circassian* Spring Meeting" would take place at eleven o'clock on Saturday forenoon had been posted up, and, there being no gate-money, a large concourse of spectators assembled. The "event" was a purely athletic one, and the "card" was well filled with entries for the various stakes, which comprised flat, hurdle, and one-legged races; chalk-the-line, egg race, tug of war, etc. The ringing of the starter's bell, firing of pistol, and clearing the course of the inevitable Derby dog, were not the least entertaining incidents of the gathering.

A grand concert in the evening—also fitly advertised, and for which elaborate programmes had been engrossed—came off with great *eclat,* the talented amateurs going through their well practised parts in capital style. An *improvisitore* created great enthusiasm by singing a song, the chorus of which was, "Oh! shan't we be sorry to leave the *Circassian,* leave *the Circassian,* leave *the Circassian*," in which everybody joined *ad. Lib.*

DAY FIFTY-NINE.

Trinity Sunday passed away in the manner to which we had now become accustomed to spend the Sabbath on the ocean; exquisite weather favouring both deck exercise and repose.

Before turning in, the bold land of the Island of Aran loomed under our starboard bow, and the bright light on Tory Island shone on the horizon far ahead.

DAY SIXTY.

To be up with the sun did not admit of a long sojourn among the blankets, and as we passed into Lough Foyle at daybreak most of us were on deck to bid good-bye to those who were going to leave us at Moville, and to get an early peep at the newspapers that would be brought on board. The tender was in waiting, and took away the London mails and the passengers for Ireland and Scotland. A trip up the Lough, of twelve miles, was before them, ere they could take train at Londonderry, or steamboat for Glasgow.

The ever-vaunted verdancy of the Irish vegetation was as striking and re-freshing as ever, after being accustomed to foreign land-scapes, which, even in the choicest spots of the American Continent, lack that peculiar green so charming in the British Isles. The appropriately-named Green Castle was the first object to take our notice, the grand old ivy-covered ruin, with its adjacent walled and trimly kept enclosure, being a fine ornament to the western point of the entrance. Spotlessly white lighthouses and keepers' residences brightened the day scene as their kindly lights had recently done the night one.

This loyal, prosperous, and happy corner of Erin, with its cosy farmsteads, country seats, and highly cultivated fields, gave our Canadian cousins who were visiting the old country for the first time a good impression of the home islands of her Majesty's dominions.

Emerging again into the open sea, we were struck with the difference in the colour of the water, now that we were "in soundings" instead of being borne upon the all but fathomless ocean of the past week.

Dunluce Castle, on our right, threw us into raptures, and our ever ready guide, philosopher and friend, the captain, assumed the post of showman, taking the ladies on to the pilot bridge, and expatiating, as only an Irishman can do, upon the glori-ous coast scenery of his native land.

The Giant's Causeway was seen to great advantage; in fact our good fortune in having all the principal sights served up for us under the best possible of circum-stances stuck to us to the last. As we steamed along within a stone's throw of the cliffs, our conductor had a rare opportunity of pointing out every feature of the interesting coast. He was able to assure us that never, in the four hundred and forty-six times that he had gone by, had he seen such a lovely aspect of the north-eastern shores of Ireland. Later on in the day the sun-light would not have been upon the face of the rocks, and earlier the details of the picture could not have been discerned in the semi-darkness of the summer night.

The singular basaltic columnar formation which is visible here is identical with that of the opposite coast at Staffa, so that the continuity of land which some ingenious minds have contemplated establishing by prolonging the Mull of Cantyre to Erin by a gigantic feat of "navvying" and engineering has patently had a pre-historic natural antecedent.

Further on we had a good view of the Mull, its height causing it to look much nearer than its actual distance of twenty miles.

But to finish with the "Causeway." Some isolated pillars presented the aspect of chimneys, and tradition says that the remnant of the Spanish Armada that drifted this way fired upon them for such. The giant's cauldron, his brandy bottle (with cork complete), his great organ, little organ, and lastly the grim monster himself, were all duly pointed out; and, need-less to say, were all *exactly* like the objects suggested—just as are the innumerable recurrences of Adam and Eve, the Twelve Apostles, and other persons and things in various parts of the world, including such veracious resemblances as the Pope and Two Nuns, and the Russian and the Turk of the Harz Mountains.

The towers of Basalt end in Fairhead, a bluff which we could almost touch, and were told that there was water deep enough for our vessel to go right up to it.

A pretty islet, Sheep Island, lay between us and a portion of the mainland; and, shutting out of our view part of the Scottish coast, was the Irish island of Rathlin, immortalized as the *locale* of Bruce's contemplation of the persevering spider in his prison cell.

Ballycastle Bay and the snug village in its indent passed to our rear as

Each sail was set And each heart was gay

and we descended to the saloon and the prosaic, well appetized for our morning refection, sailing upon a sea which laved the shores of England, Wales, Scotland, and Ireland.

The Isle of Man was passed at the Calf; and soon the hills of North Wales came in sight, the crest of Snowdon cutting the sky line in the background.

At eight o'clock we were at the Mersey bar lightship, our ***point d'appui*** of two months before; and, after lying for a few hours at anchor waiting for the tide we crossed the bar within an hour of sixty days from the commencement of our scamper of close upon fifteen thousand miles, having traversed new ground or water for almost every mile of it; consecutive travelling stated by a competent authority to be unprecedented; and, as far as a lady's wanderings were concerned, it was so beyond all doubt.

FINISH.

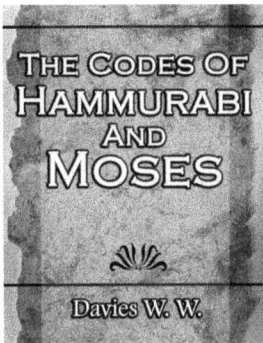

The Codes Of Hammurabi And Moses
W. W. Davies

QTY

The discovery of the Hammurabi Code is one of the greatest achievements of archaeology, and is of paramount interest, not only to the student of the Bible, but also to all those interested in ancient history...

Religion   **ISBN:** *1-59462-338-4*   **Pages:132**
MSRP $12.95

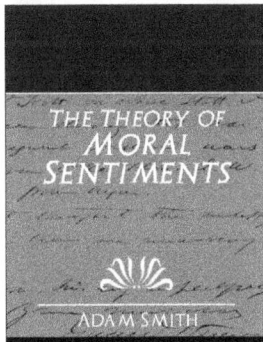

The Theory of Moral Sentiments
Adam Smith

QTY

This work from 1749. contains original theories of conscience amd moral judgment and it is the foundation for systemof morals.

Philosophy **ISBN:** *1-59462-777-0*   **Pages:536**
MSRP $19.95

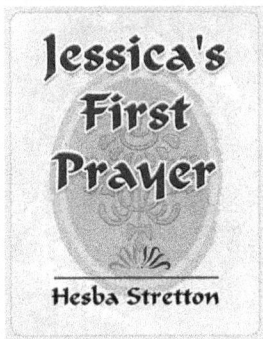

Jessica's First Prayer
Hesba Stretton

QTY

In a screened and secluded corner of one of the many railway-bridges which span the streets of London there could be seen a few years ago, from five o'clock every morning until half past eight, a tidily set-out coffee-stall, consisting of a trestle and board, upon which stood two large tin cans, with a small fire of charcoal burning under each so as to keep the coffee boiling during the early hours of the morning when the work-people were thronging into the city on their way to their daily toil...

Childrens   **ISBN:** *1-59462-373-2*   **Pages:84**
MSRP $9.95

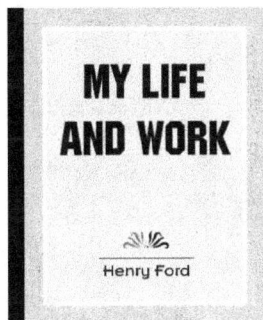

My Life and Work
Henry Ford

QTY

Henry Ford revolutionized the world with his implementation of mass production for the Model T automobile. Gain valuable business insight into his life and work with his own auto-biography... "We have only started on our development of our country we have not as yet, with all our talk of wonderful progress, done more than scratch the surface. The progress has been wonderful enough but..."

Biographies/ **ISBN:** *1-59462-198-5*   **Pages:300**
MSRP $21.95

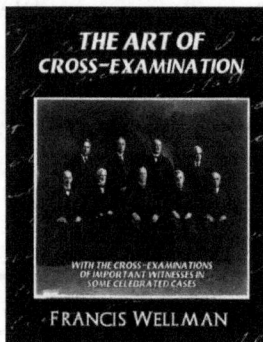

The Art of Cross-Examination
Francis Wellman

QTY

I presume it is the experience of every author, after his first book is published upon an important subject, to be almost overwhelmed with a wealth of ideas and illustrations which could readily have been included in his book, and which to his own mind, at least, seem to make a second edition inevitable. Such certainly was the case with me; and when the first edition had reached its sixth impression in five months, I rejoiced to learn that it seemed to my publishers that the book had met with a sufficiently favorable reception to justify a second and considerably enlarged edition. ..

Pages:412

Reference   ISBN: *1-59462-647-2*   *MSRP $19.95*

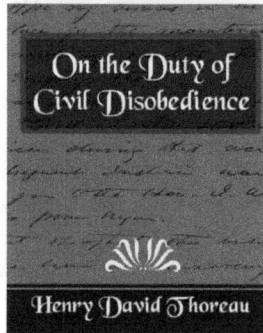

On the Duty of Civil Disobedience
Henry David Thoreau

QTY

Thoreau wrote his famous essay, On the Duty of Civil Disobedience, as a protest against an unjust but popular war and the immoral but popular institution of slave-owning. He did more than write—he declined to pay his taxes, and was hauled off to gaol in consequence. Who can say how much this refusal of his hastened the end of the war and of slavery ?

Pages:48

Law   ISBN: *1-59462-747-9*   *MSRP $7.45*

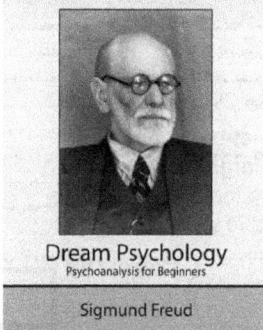

Dream Psychology Psychoanalysis for Beginners
Sigmund Freud

QTY

Sigmund Freud, born Sigismund Schlomo Freud (May 6, 1856 - September 23, 1939), was a Jewish-Austrian neurologist and psychiatrist who co-founded the psychoanalytic school of psychology. Freud is best known for his theories of the unconscious mind, especially involving the mechanism of repression; his redefinition of sexual desire as mobile and directed towards a wide variety of objects; and his therapeutic techniques, especially his understanding of transference in the therapeutic relationship and the presumed value of dreams as sources of insight into unconscious desires.

Pages:196

Psychology   ISBN: *1-59462-905-6*   *MSRP $15.45*

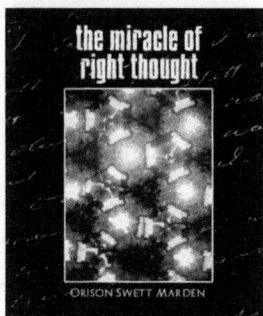

The Miracle of Right Thought
Orison Swett Marden

QTY

Believe with all of your heart that you will do what you were made to do. When the mind has once formed the habit of holding cheerful, happy, prosperous pictures, it will not be easy to form the opposite habit. It does not matter how improbable or how far away this realization may see, or how dark the prospects may be, if we visualize them as best we can, as vividly as possible, hold tenaciously to them and vigorously struggle to attain them, they will gradually become actualized, realized in the life. But a desire, a longing without endeavor, a yearning abandoned or held indifferently will vanish without realization.

Pages:360

Self Help   ISBN: *1-59462-644-8*   *MSRP $25.45*

QTY

The Rosicrucian Cosmo-Conception Mystic Christianity *by Max Heindel*   ISBN: *1-59462-188-8*   **$38.95**
The Rosicrucian Cosmo-conception is not dogmatic, neither does it appeal to any other authority than the reason of the student. It is: not controversial, but is: sent forth in the, hope that it may help to clear...   *New Age/Religion Pages 646*

Abandonment To Divine Providence *by Jean-Pierre de Caussade*   ISBN: *1-59462-228-0*   **$25.95**
"The Rev. Jean Pierre de Caussade was one of the most remarkable spiritual writers of the Society of Jesus in France in the 18th Century. His death took place at Toulouse in 1751. His works have gone through many editions and have been republished...   *Inspirational/Religion Pages 400*

Mental Chemistry *by Charles Haanel*   ISBN: *1-59462-192-6*   **$23.95**
Mental Chemistry allows the change of material conditions by combining and appropriately utilizing the power of the mind. Much like applied chemistry creates something new and unique out of careful combinations of chemicals the mastery of mental chemistry...   *New Age Pages 354*

The Letters of Robert Browning and Elizabeth Barret Barrett 1845-1846 vol II   ISBN: *1-59462-193-4*   **$35.95**
by Robert Browning and Elizabeth Barrett   *Biographies Pages 596*

Gleanings In Genesis (volume I) *by Arthur W. Pink*   ISBN: *1-59462-130-6*   **$27.45**
Appropriately has Genesis been termed "the seed plot of the Bible" for in it we have, in germ form, almost all of the great doctrines which are afterwards fully developed in the books of Scripture which follow...   *Religion/Inspirational Pages 420*

The Master Key *by L. W. de Laurence*   ISBN: *1-59462-001-6*   **$30.95**
In no branch of human knowledge has there been a more lively increase of the spirit of research during the past few years than in the study of Psychology, Concentration and Mental Discipline. The requests for authentic lessons in Thought Control, Mental Discipline and...   *New Age/Business Pages 422*

The Lesser Key Of Solomon Goetia *by L. W. de Laurence*   ISBN: *1-59462-092-X*   **$9.95**
This translation of the first book of the "Lernegton" which is now for the first time made accessible to students of Talismanic Magic was done, after careful collation and edition, from numerous Ancient Manuscripts in Hebrew, Latin, and French...   *New Age/Occult Pages 92*

Rubaiyat Of Omar Khayyam *by Edward Fitzgerald*   ISBN: *1-59462-332-5*   **$13.95**
Edward Fitzgerald, whom the world has already learned, in spite of his own efforts to remain within the shadow of anonymity, to look upon as one of the rarest poets of the century, was born at Bredfield, in Suffolk, on the 31st of March, 1809. He was the third son of John Purcell...   *Music Pages 172*

Ancient Law *by Henry Maine*   ISBN: *1-59462-128-4*   **$29.95**
The chief object of the following pages is to indicate some of the earliest ideas of mankind, as they are reflected in Ancient Law, and to point out the relation of those ideas to modern thought.   *Religion/History Pages 452*

Far-Away Stories *by William J. Locke*   ISBN: *1-59462-129-2*   **$19.45**
"Good wine needs no bush, but a collection of mixed vintages does. And this book is just such a collection. Some of the stories I do not want to remain buried for ever in the museum files of dead magazine-numbers an author's not unpardonable vanity..."   *Fiction Pages 272*

Life of David Crockett *by David Crockett*   ISBN: *1-59462-250-7*   **$27.45**
"Colonel David Crockett was one of the most remarkable men of the times in which he lived. Born in humble life, but gifted with a strong will, an indomitable courage, and unremitting perseverance...   *Biographies/New Age Pages 424*

Lip-Reading *by Edward Nitchie*   ISBN: *1-59462-206-X*   **$25.95**
Edward B. Nitchie, founder of the New York School for the Hard of Hearing, now the Nitchie School of Lip-Reading, Inc, wrote "LIP-READING Principles and Practice". The development and perfecting of this meritorious work on lip-reading was an undertaking...   *How-to Pages 400*

A Handbook of Suggestive Therapeutics, Applied Hypnotism, Psychic Science   ISBN: *1-59462-214-0*   **$24.95**
by Henry Munro   *Health/New Age/Health/Self-help Pages 376*

A Doll's House: and Two Other Plays *by Henrik Ibsen*   ISBN: *1-59462-112-8*   **$19.95**
Henrik Ibsen created this classic when in revolutionary 1848 Rome. Introducing some striking concepts in playwriting for the realist genre, this play has been studied the world over.   *Fiction/Classics/Plays 308*

The Light of Asia *by sir Edwin Arnold*   ISBN: *1-59462-204-3*   **$13.95**
In this poetic masterpiece, Edwin Arnold describes the life and teachings of Buddha. The man who was to become known as Buddha to the world was born as Prince Gautama of India but he rejected the worldly riches and abandoned the reigns of power when...   *Religion/History/Biographies Pages 170*

The Complete Works of Guy de Maupassant *by Guy de Maupassant*   ISBN: *1-59462-157-8*   **$16.95**
"For days and days, nights and nights, I had dreamed of that first kiss which was to consecrate our engagement, and I knew not on what spot I should put my lips..."   *Fiction/Classics Pages 240*

The Art of Cross-Examination *by Francis L. Wellman*   ISBN: *1-59462-309-0*   **$26.95**
Written by a renowned trial lawyer, Wellman imparts his experience and uses case studies to explain how to use psychology to extract desired information through questioning.   *How-to/Science/Reference Pages 408*

Answered or Unanswered? *by Louisa Vaughan*   ISBN: *1-59462-248-5*   **$10.95**
Miracles of Faith in China   *Religion Pages 112*

The Edinburgh Lectures on Mental Science (1909) *by Thomas*   ISBN: *1-59462-008-3*   **$11.95**
This book contains the substance of a course of lectures recently given by the writer in the Queen Street Hall, Edinburgh. Its purpose is to indicate the Natural Principles governing the relation between Mental Action and Material Conditions...   *New Age/Psychology Pages 148*

Ayesha *by H. Rider Haggard*   ISBN: *1-59462-301-5*   **$24.95**
Verily and indeed it is the unexpected that happens! Probably if there was one person upon the earth from whom the Editor of this, and of a certain previous history, did not expect to hear again...   *Classics Pages 380*

Ayala's Angel *by Anthony Trollope*   ISBN: *1-59462-352-X*   **$29.95**
The two girls were both pretty, but Lucy who was twenty-one who supposed to be simple and comparatively unattractive, whereas Ayala was credited, as her Bombwhat romantic name might show, with poetic charm and a taste for romance. Ayala when her father died was nineteen...   *Fiction Pages 484*

The American Commonwealth *by James Bryce*   ISBN: *1-59462-286-8*   **$34.45**
An interpretation of American democratic political theory. It examines political mechanics and society from the perspective of Scotsman James Bryce   *Politics Pages 572*

Stories of the Pilgrims *by Margaret P. Pumphrey*   ISBN: *1-59462-116-0*   **$17.95**
This book explores pilgrims religious oppression in England as well as their escape to Holland and eventual crossing to America on the Mayflower, and their early days in New England...   *History Pages 268*

QTY

The Fasting Cure *by Sinclair Upton*   ISBN: *1-59462-222-1* **$13.95**
*In the Cosmopolitan Magazine for May, 1910, and in the Contemporary Review (London) for April, 1910, I published an article dealing with my experi-
ences in fasting. I have written a great many magazine articles, but never one which attracted so much attention... New Age/Self Help/Health Pages 164*

Hebrew Astrology *by Sepharial*   ISBN: *1-59462-308-2* **$13.45**
*In these days of advanced thinking it is a matter of common observation that we have left many of the old landmarks behind and that we are now pressing
forward to greater heights and to a wider horizon than that which represented the mind-content of our progenitors...   Astrology Pages 144*

Thought Vibration or The Law of Attraction in the Thought World   ISBN: *1-59462-127-6* **$12.95**
by William Walker Atkinson   *Psychology/Religion Pages 144*

Optimism *by Helen Keller*   ISBN: *1-59462-108-X* **$15.95**
*Helen Keller was blind, deaf, and mute since 19 months old, yet famously learned how to overcome these handicaps, communicate with the world, and
spread her lectures promoting optimism. An inspiring read for everyone...   Biographies/Inspirational Pages 84*

Sara Crewe *by Frances Burnett*   ISBN: *1-59462-360-0*   **$9.45**
*In the first place, Miss Minchin lived in London. Her home was a large, dull, tall one, in a large, dull square, where all the houses were alike, and all the
sparrows were alike, and where all the door-knockers made the same heavy sound...   Childrens/Classic Pages 88*

The Autobiography of Benjamin Franklin *by Benjamin Franklin*   ISBN: *1-59462-135-7* **$24.95**
*The Autobiography of Benjamin Franklin has probably been more extensively read than any other American historical work, and no other book of its kind
has had such ups and downs of fortune. Franklin lived for many years in England, where he was agent...   Biographies/History Pages 332*

Name	
Email	
Telephone	
Address	
City, State ZIP	

☐ **Credit Card**   ☐ **Check / Money Order**

Credit Card Number	
Expiration Date	
Signature	

*Please Mail to: Book Jungle
                   PO Box 2226
                   Champaign, IL 61825*
      or Fax to: 630-214-0564

www.ingramcontent.com/pod-product-compliance
Lightning Source LLC
Chambersburg PA
CBHW081232090426
42738CB00016B/3272